Win More Union Organizing Drives

BY
Jason Mann

INTRODUCTION

"Promoting Your Union" outlined six of the best strategies for unions to reach out to non-union workers to get more and better organizing leads.[1]

This book covers the next stage in the process: turning those leads into organized workplaces.

If we want to increase the number of workers organized our two options are:

- Increase the resources spent on organizing
- Win a higher percentage of organizing drives

While both of these approaches are necessary, only one is directly in the control of union organizers: winning more union organizing drives.

Here are examples of the ideas you'll find in this book:

"If you do all the work for your committee then you are cheating them out of the lessons they need to learn about how to stand together and win."
– *Chapter Four, Building Inside Committees*

"What is written on a leaflet isn't as important as who is handing it out and whose picture is on it."
- *Chapter Five, Communicating Our Message*

"Recognize card signing for what it is. Card signing isn't the

---

[1] You can download a free video training series that outlines the strategies in the book at http://www.PromotingYourUnion.com

organizing drive itself – it is a stage of the campaign necessary to get the union that you help build legally recognized."
– *Chapter Six, Card Signing Campaign*

"Union organizing isn't about cards – it's about relationships. House calls allow you to build the relationships needed to win the election, strike vote and first collective agreement."
– *Chapter Seven, House Calls*

"The best protection working people have isn't the labour board, it is each other. "
– *Chapter Eight, Winning the Boss Fight*

"Very few people actually join a union for the sake of trade unionism itself. It isn't that they've always wanted to be a union member and finally the chance has come. It is almost always the concrete conditions they face at the workplace. Your job as an organizer is to help find these concrete conditions and find the triggers which will make the difference in a vote."
– *Chapter Nine, Using Bargaining Surveys*

"If a union is built from the outside, then it doesn't belong to the workers from the very beginning – and if they didn't build it, they aren't very likely to keep it either."
– *Chapter Ten, Acting Like a Union*

"The more time an employer spends on responding to your external campaign, the less time they have to interfere in the process dealing with whether or not workers should join a union."
– *Chapter Eleven, The External Campaign*

"The greatest factor in winning a vote isn't the tactics you use

on the day of the vote, but what you have done every day up until the day of the vote."
– Chapter Twelve, Winning Elections

"Great follow-up systems are systematic. They don't rely on an organizer remembering to pull open a file from an unsuccessful campaign. They maintain the relationship 24/7, not just when the organizer runs out of organizing leads."
– Chapter Thirteen, Followup Campaigns

"People want to contribute. They want to be a part of something. They want to have ownership. These are all things that people can get by being a member organizer that they can't get from attending a membership meeting." – Chapter Fourteen, Involving Members in Organizing Drives

In the long run increasing the win rate of organizing drives also helps in the political fight to allocate more resources to organizing.

Academic studies on union organizing have estimated that unions spend between $1300-$2700 on every member they successfully organize.

Doubling the percentage of campaigns that leads to a win not only means organizing twice as many workers, but it also means doubling the return on money spent on union organizing.

If increasing organizing spending will organize twice as many workers, it makes increased organizing spending easier to justify.

The purpose of this book is to spread best practices and encourage unions to focus on improving their win rates on campaigns.

This book is divided accorded to campaign stages:

BEFORE THE CAMPAIGN
- Targeting and Benchmarks
- Creating Comprehensive Campaign Plans
- Record Keeping

DURING THE CAMPAIGN
- Building Representative Inside Committees
- Communicating Our Message
- Card Signing Campaign
- House Calls
- Winning the Boss Fight
- Using Bargaining Surveys
- Acting Like a Union
- External Campaigns
- Winning Elections

AFTER THE CAMPAIGN
- Follow-up Campaigns
- Involving Members in Campaigns
- Learning From Campaigns

Because many of the strategies to increase win rates are best practices, this book could also be used as a training manual for new organizers.

For experienced organizers, my hope is that you will find one good strategy that can help make a difference in your union.

CHAPTER ONE: TARGETING AND BENCHMARKS

The easiest and fastest way for your union to improve its organizing win rate is to select better targets.

The goal of the labour movement should be to bring collective bargaining to all working people. But that doesn't mean that the fastest way to get there is to organize everyone at once or make organizing decisions based on who walks into our office.

To win more union organizing drives the labour movement must be focused and disciplined with the types of campaigns we run.

The fastest way for us to get to a point where every worker has a union is to make sure the campaigns we are taking on are a good fit for our union and organizing team at the particular time.

A survey of NLRB elections found that unions that organized units that were part of a researched targeting plan had an election win rate of 51% compared to a 41% win rate for unions that did not use strategic targeting.[2]

Conservatively assuming that the average organizing cost is $1000 per worker successfully organized, the cost to your union to successfully organize a 75 person worksite is $75,000.

---

[2] Throughout this book references to win rates come from surveys of NLRB elections by Kate Bronfenbrenner and Robert Hickey. You can find the theoretical models, statistical significance of figures, and sum of squared residuals etc in the original research.

Treat the decision where to start a campaign as seriously as you would take a decision to spend $75,000.

When new organizing leads come your way you should ask yourself questions like:

- Does this unit have strategic importance to our local and current membership?

- Does it increase our bargaining power?

- Is this a unit that we can hold onto for several years?

- Is this an industry that is growing or dying?

- Is the unit size a good match for our union, both in terms of servicing and organizing capacity?

In surveys of NLRB elections, campaigns that assigned one organizer for every 100 eligible voters in the unit; one woman organizer for units with 25% or more women; and one organizer of color for units with 25% or more workers of color had win rates of 64% compared to a 41% win rate for campaigns that attempted to organize units that were not a good fit for their organizing capacity.

SETTING CAMPAIGN BENCHMARKS

Unions that use a formalized system for benchmarks and assessments for proceeding with the campaigns have higher win rates than those who do not.

While only a quarter of the campaigns surveyed used benchmarks and assessments, those campaigns were responsible for 35% of NLRB wins.

Campaigns that used benchmarking and formal assessments had a win rate of 66% compared to a 38% win rate for campaigns that relied on the organizers' gut instincts without using benchmarks and assessments.

Just having a checklist of how to proceed with campaigns could improve your win rate by 31 percentage points.

DO BENCHMARKS MAKE SENSE FOR EXPERIENCED ORGANIZERS?

An organizer may be hesitant about having formal benchmarks for campaign decisions because instead they feel that these decisions are best left to their gut.

Here's the reason why organizers with great judgment and years of organizing experience should use benchmarks for decision making: *Benchmark systems protect the integrity of your decision.*

Let's say that you've been working on a campaign at a strategic target for nearly a year. It took time to get a full employee list and to build up a fully representative inside committee before you started signing cards. You're making progress in card signing, and you've finally signing up 55% of the worksite.

But the union leadership is impatient.

They start saying things like: "Lets put it to a vote, if we win, we win; and if we lose then we probably couldn't organize the place anyway."

Having a system of benchmarks allows you to protect your decision making and say, "Our organizing department has a standard benchmark of having 60% of cards signed and positive momentum before filing because it is the best way to be successful."

INSIDE COMMITTEE PRESSURE

We've all heard inside committee members say, "I know people aren't signing cards, but I'm absolutely sure that they are going to vote 'yes' if there is an election."

The way to avoid a disagreement with your inside committee about campaign strategy is to educate your inside committee on the campaign milestones they must reach on their way to forming their union.

Tell the inside committee right up front that you aren't going to start signing cards until they have 10% of the workplace on the inside committee.

Tell them that you aren't going to file until you have at least 60% of cards signed, not just the minimum to file.

If you establish these benchmarks up front, you'll find that your committee will be much less likely to push the campaign to a loss because of impatience.

WHAT TO BENCHMARK

If setting benchmarks is an easy way to ensure that you win more organizing drives, what type of benchmarks should your organizing department set during a campaign?

You should have benchmarks for:

- Inside Committees
- Card Signing

- Filing applications

INSIDE COMMITTEE BENCHMARKS

The organizing team should have standard benchmarks for deciding when to move from the 'building the inside committee' stage to the 'card signing' stage.

When your card signing dries up in a campaign, it is almost always because you didn't identify and recruit all of the leaders.

The time to recruit leaders is before you're out in the open signing cards and up against the employer's campaign.

Additionally, your inside committee should be representative of the workplace.

Ensure that your committee reflects language groups, gender balance, and departments.

There are two main reasons to have benchmarks for your inside committee.

1. SETTING EXPECTATIONS

Forming a union is a new experience for your inside committee:

Having benchmarks gives them the positive re-enforcement that they are doing well or a reality check that they need to get serious about their effort.

2. TRANSITIONING OUT OF UNSUCCESSFUL CAMPAIGNS

Often the timing isn't right for a campaign. Sometimes the

right thing to do is back down and come back later rather than pushing all out towards a loss.

If you come to an inside committee meeting and tell them you are scaling back the campaign, they may be resentful because they feel they are doing well. If your inside committee doesn't agree with your decision then they aren't going to rejoin your committee the next time you try to organize the workplace.

However if you establish criteria to move forward or pull back ahead of time, your inside committee will be more likely to help when you come back to organize the workplace.

APPLICATION FOR CERTIFICATION BENCHMARKS

There are two sets of benchmarks to set for proceeding with an application:

1. CARDS SIGNED

Aim to have at least 60% of cards signed prior to filing a certification application. Generally through employer interference, your support level will drop by 10 percentage points. To have a shot at getting 50% at the vote, you can't go in with less than 60% of cards signed at the application.

2. POSITIVE MOMENTUM

If you are losing momentum at the workplace, it isn't the correct time to file, even if you have 60% of cards signed.

BENCHMARKS FOR LISTS

Wal-Mart has a policy preventing employees from telling co-workers their last name.

You're on a first name basis only. After all, it's all one big family!

The truth of the matter is that Wal-Mart knows the importance of having a complete employee list prior to starting an organizing drive.

While setting a benchmark for a complete list prior to starting card signing is tough, here are a few reasons why you should consider setting such a high bar:

1. IT IS A PRACTICAL TEST OF YOUR INSIDE COMMITTEE

If your inside committee doesn't have the connections to put together a list of the people who work in a particular department, they probably don't have the connections to sign up the department either.

This is often an indication that you need to broaden your committee so that it is more reflective of the workplace.

2. IT IS EASIER NOW THAN LATER

The second reason to have a full employee list before you start the card signing campaign is that it is easier to bring your inside committee onboard with creating a list near the beginning of the campaign than when you are in the heat of card signing.

3. CONTROL THE CAMPAIGN PACE

When you have a full list you can control the momentum and tempo of the campaign. Sometimes it is advantageous to step up the pace of a campaign and other times you'll want to pace yourself.

If you don't have a list before you start card signing, the lack of the list will dictate your campaign tempo.

4. LEGAL EXPENSES

Often having full and complete information can be essential to proceeding with legal challenges quickly or avoiding them entirely.

CHAPTER TWO: COMPREHENSIVE CAMPAIGN PLANS

Campaigns that use a variety of tactics and multifaceted approaches to organize have higher win rates.

A survey of NLRB elections found that organizing drives that only used a single tactic had a win rate in elections of 28%.

The same survey found over a third of the campaigns they reviewed used only one approach in their campaign.

Unions that ran a slightly better campaign and used two tactics had a win rate of 47%.

That is an improvement of almost 20 percentage points.

Campaigns that used 7 or more approaches and tactics had a win rate of 70%.

Campaigns that combined, for example, an external campaign, member organizers, house calls, an internal campaign, benchmarking, strategic targeting, and a bargaining survey won almost every single time. Unfortunately comprehensive campaigns that use 7 tactics or more made up only 2% of total organizing drives in the survey.

CAMPAIGN STRATEGY CHECKLIST

One of the easiest ways to increase your win rate is to put together a campaign strategy checklist to evaluate your campaign plan.

The checklist should be prepared by the lead organizer and be signed-off by the organizing director or president prior to the launch of any new organizing campaign.

Organizers should demonstrate that they have a plan for the campaign, what they are going to do, when, and how they will evaluate their campaign.

Remember, the cost of successfully organizing a single worker is $1000. Before allocating that kind of money, organizers should back up the campaign with a plan.

The campaign checklist forces organizers to go through the process of reviewing all of the best practices associated with winning more organizing drives.

WHY PLAN?

Many of the best practices of organizing require planning and preparation. For example doing community work or an external campaign as part of your organizing drive, means that there is research to do in advance.

Some campaigns better lend themselves to certain tactics.

It may not make sense for a campaign at a 20-person worksite to incorporate a community strategy.

But if you aren't going to do an external campaign, you should consider what you should do instead to make sure that you are running as comprehensive a campaign as possible.

COST OBJECTION

But wait, isn't it more expensive to run full comprehensive campaigns using a variety of tactics?

Yes, it takes more time too, but losing organizing drives because of low win rates is even more expensive and wastes even more time.

CAMPAIGN CHECKLISTS PROTECT YOUR ORGANIZING DRIVE

Your campaign plan should have a series of benchmarks based on best practices.

Objective criteria for managing your campaign tactics protects your campaign from pressure from above or hasty decisions made by your inside committee.

Your plan should have approximate dates for setting up your inside committee, timelines for cards, and when you expect to have 10, 40,60% of the unit signed up. When do you expect to be able to file? How much staff time do you expect to require for different stages of the campaign?

CHAPTER THREE: KEEPING RECORDS AND TRACKING COMMITMENTS

What does having a good database and record keeping system have to do with winning more organizing campaigns?

1. ORGANIZER TURN OVER

Organizers have a higher turnover rate than other position in your union.

Because of the high turnover rates among union organizers, leaving all of the information of your campaigns solely in the head of the lead organizer isn't a good plan.

2. TEAMWORK

Recording levels of support, notes from conversations and each interaction with a worker allows for team approaches to organizing.

Organizers that work collectively have better win rates on larger campaigns than those run by individual organizers alone.

Increasing the number of non-union workers we reach means taking on the same number of campaigns at larger worksites, or taking on more campaigns. Either approach requires better organization and record keeping.

3. FOLLOW-UP SYSTEMS

A contact management system (also known as a customer

relationship system or CRM) allows you to follow up with commitments to make sure people follow through.

So if your inside committee member tells you that she is going to talk with someone on a certain date, you need to be able to track that commitment and check if it was followed up.

This not only helps you follow up with someone, it ensures that other people haven't already been assigned to speak with that person.

4. FUTURE CAMPAIGNS

Not all organizing drives are won the first time around.

An employee list alone doesn't give you enough information to put together a solid second campaign.

It is helpful to also know:

- What were the issues in the last campaign?
- What were issues of specific individuals?
- Who knew whom in the workplace?
- Who was most successful at signing up cards on your inside committee?
- What reasons did people give for not signing cards?

This is all critical information to ensure that your next organizing drive takes off.

5. DELIVERING THE RIGHT MESSAGE TO THE RIGHT PEOPLE

CRMs give you the ability to personalize and microtarget your communications to individual workers.

If the workplace has employees with a variety of first languages, then personalize your messages to make sure you can easily send a message in the right language to the right person.

WHAT TO TRACK IN YOUR RECORD KEEPING SYSTEM

Your records should contain more information than simply if a card was signed.

Consider tracking:

- Language
- Important issues
- Organizer assigned to contact
- Inside committee member assigned to contact
- Contact information
- Is someone a leader?
- Did someone sign a card?
- Have they been asked to sign a card?
- What day they signed a card?
- Gender
- Ethnicity

- Department
- Employment status
- Previous conversations
- Level of support

Some example benefits of using computer record keeping systems:

If you track the date a worker signs a card you can automatically print out a list of cards that will expire in the next two weeks.

You can run reports that help you make decisions on campaign scenarios.

I.e.: If you intend to file for certification in two weeks, how many card signers will you have by that point?

If you track employment status and department you can quickly see what happens if certain groups are excluded or included in your certification.

Better information leads to better campaign decisions. Better campaign decisions lead to better win rates.

Knowing that you've signed 10 workers out of 100 after two weeks doesn't give you enough information to make campaign decisions. But knowing that after two weeks of campaigning you've reached 40% of workers, with only 10 signing cards and the rest opposed is a completely different scenario.

These are all things you cannot do efficiently with a paper

system.

SETTING UP A 1-5 MARKING SYSTEM

The most common way to measure a worker's support for a union is a 1 to 5 scale.

The important part of a 1 to 5 marking system is that it can't be based on feelings. It must be based on objective criteria.

It should be based on things like:

- Has someone signed a card?
- Are they willing to come to inside committee meetings?
- Are they willing to tell you about issues they are having at work?
- Are the objections they raise genuine questions?

DESIGNING A 1-5 MARKING SYSTEM

1's are strong union supporters.

2's are people leaning towards the union.

3's are people who are undecided.

4's are people leaning away from the union.

5's are people who are thoroughly anti-union.

It's also worth recording who the leaders in a workplace are.

A conversation with a 2L, a leader leaning towards a union, is a different conversation than you'd have with 1, a non leader supporter of the union.

When estimating the result of a vote that was held at a workplace, one of the most accurate ways to do this is to add up your 1's and 2's and subtract your 3's, 4's and 5's.

A positive number indicates a likely win; negative numbers indicate a loss.

CHAPTER FOUR: BUILDING REPRESENTATIVE INSIDE COMMITTEES

HOW INSIDE COMMITTEES AFFECT WIN RATES

Only 25% of organizing drives that make it to a vote actually have fully developed and representative inside committees.

The impact on win rates between campaigns that have fully developed inside committees and those that do not is substantial.

The win rate for campaigns with inside committees was 56%.

The quarter of campaigns that had fully developed inside committees made up 33% of all successful elections.

The win rate for the 75% of campaigns that did not have fully developed inside committees was 41%. Over a 10 point difference.

WHAT ARE THE KEYS TO RECRUITING A LARGE INSIDE COMMITTEE?

It can be hard to recruit 10% of the workforce to the inside committee.

Here are some of the keys:

1. SET EXPECTATIONS EARLY

From the first meeting, you must make the tasks of the inside committee clear.

Your contact may be under the impression that they call the union, and then a paid staff person comes out – makes a bunch of phone calls, and soon they'll walk away with a union contract and a hefty pay increase.

The reality is that it is their union – and no one can build it for them.

If you set expectations at the beginning, the committee will be more likely to help you recruit the inside committee later in the campaign.

2. NO CARD SIGNING UNTIL THERE IS A COMMITTEE

Not starting the card signing process until you have a fully developed inside committee encourages your committee to take building the committee seriously.

Card signing is exciting. Once they start the process of card signing, all of their focus will be on getting new cards, not continuing to build and strengthen the committee.

3. ASK FOR REFERRALS

When doing house calls early in the campaign, ask workers who else they think should join the inside committee.

- Who would they like to see helping out?
- Who do they consider a trustworthy person?
- Who is highly respected at the workplace?
- Who is a leader?
- Who stands up for their co-workers?

Often you need to provoke existing committee members with these questions so they don't end up an inside committee that represents only a close group of friends at the worksite.

4. ASK PEOPLE TO COME OUT AND PROVIDE INPUT

The easiest way to convince someone to take part in the inside committee is to ask for their input.

"I've had a few people suggest to me that you are a person that should be involved in the process. It sounds like you are well respected by your other co-workers. I thought it would be valuable if we could get your input at the next meeting."

Most people don't like the idea of "joining committees", but they do like the idea of providing input and feeling valued.

WHAT SHOULD YOUR INSIDE COMMITTEE LOOK LIKE?

There are three things that give your inside committee power: Leadership, representation and diversity.

1. LEADERSHIP

Campaigns can be won or lost depending on who gets to the workplace leaders first: you or the union buster.

When card signing dries up, it is generally because you haven't found all of the workplace leaders in a particular department.

Workplace leaders appreciate if you come to them sooner than later.

2. REPRESENTATION

Management pits workers against one another to undermine their solidarity.

Not only are you potentially missing out on cards and feedback from groups not represented on the inside committee, but their exclusion might actually cause people to resent the union and the inside committee.

If front desk staff don't see themselves reflected in an organizing drive at a hotel, it is easy for hotel management to say, "This is really more to do with housekeepers".

3. DIVERSITY

The final thing that gives an inside committee strength is it's diversity.

If the committee is completely homogeneous, it doesn't have the ability to relate with all workers at a unit and won't have much power.

In fact a smaller but more diverse inside committee often has more power than a larger homogeneous committee.

Your committee must reflect the diversity of the workplace. It must be representative of gender, language, ethnicity, and nationality to gain a variety of perspectives and have complete information to run your organizing campaign.

INSIDE COMMITTEE PITFALLS

There are a few mistakes to avoid when you are putting together your inside committee.

1. LACK OF TRAINING

As organizers, we have run so many campaigns that we

sometimes take the most basic tasks, like how to ask someone to sign a union card, for granted.

We take for granted that an individual should work off a list, map out shifts and systematically approach their co-workers based on suspected level of support.

Inside committee members may want to help, but may not know how to be most effective.

2. DOING THE WORK FOR THEM

You may be able to do a task quicker and perhaps better than your inside committee members, but this is short term thinking.

In the long run, if you do all the work for your committee, you are cheating them out of the lessons they need to learn about how to stand together and win.

3. VALUING CARDS OVER COMMITTEE

A third mistake is to think, "If I can get the cards without an inside committee, why go through the work?"

You may be able to get the cards from a unit, but will they be able to stand together without a committee when management starts their campaign?

Once I was involved in a campaign to organize a Wal-Mart store in a small union town. The strategy was to mobilize the support of the town first and then do a blitz to sign up the store with the help of our committee allies. We had a few contacts in the store but did not want to set up a full committee as we planned to sign up the store in a week and thought we couldn't risk having our plan exposed in advance.

Our campaign started with radio ads, and a mail piece sent to every house in town. We went through local union workplaces, finding people who had sons, daughters, wives, and husbands who worked at Wal-Mart.

The cards and contacts started to roll in, and much faster than we had expected they would.

It appeared that we'd have a majority of the store signed up in time to put in an application by Friday.

Then Wal-Mart moved a section of its full-time staff to part-time status and dismissed a few part-time workers.

It had a chilling effect. Card signing came to a halt.

We had card signers that were giving us information, but we had no one to testify at the labour board, ending the campaign.

4. NOT KEEPING COMMITTEE MEMBERS IN THE LOOP

The best way to keep your inside committee active and motivated is to make them insiders and constantly provide them with the inside scoop.

A time may come when you'll have to make a campaign decision quickly that just can't wait for an inside committee meeting.

If your committee isn't kept in the loop, they'll be resentful.

This lesson was demonstrated to me in a story from another organizer.

He'd been working on an organizing drive at one of his union's strategic targets. The organizing drive was hitting a wall and wasn't hitting the campaign benchmarks needed to continue. It was time to scale back the campaign to make sure they didn't leave burnt turf with a loss.

It was the correct decision based on the situation.

Unfortunately, he hadn't told the inside committee that there was a campaign timeline and benchmarks.

Despite almost no progress in building a strong committee or signing cards, the committee strongly disagreed with the idea of scaling back the campaign

The union was unable to come back later and start an inside committee because the original inside committee had no interest in working with the union organizer a second time.

WHY WAIT TO BUILD AN INSIDE COMMITTEE IF YOU CAN GET CARDS

It is worth spending time on setting up the inside committee fully before moving towards card signing.

Any organizer can go out and sign up 25% of any workplace. The challenge is signing up the next 25%, and to do that, you'll need a strong inside committee.

If you move forward with card signing prior to fully building your inside committee, you run the risk of alienating other leaders at the workplace who were not approached about joining the committee.

If they feel left out of the process and are left to wonder why the union didn't ask them, they will be harder to recruit to the inside committee later in the campaign when you'll need them.

A second reason to fully build the inside committee before you move to the card signing stage is that it is easier to recruit someone to an inside committee before the card campaign starts.

Once the cards are going around the workplace, management will step up their campaign and workers may be more afraid to join the inside committee.

It is easier for committee members to get involved before the pressure from the boss starts.

WHAT MAKES A GOOD INSIDE COMMITTEE AGENDA

There are four items that should go on your inside committee agenda: Reports, union campaign, employer campaign, and education.

1. REPORTS (OBJECTIVE SITUATION)

Start off the meeting by going around the table and reviewing previous assignments.

Inside committee members should report on what they are hearing around the workplace.

Finally do a run down of the key benchmarks of your campaign: How is card signing in each department? How are you progressing towards your inside committee building goals? Etc.

2. UNION CAMPAIGN (ASSIGNMENTS)

Next week's assignments should flow naturally from a report on last week's assignments.

Based on what you know now – where should the campaign be heading?

3. EMPLOYER CAMPAIGN (INOCULATION)

This is an opportunity to inoculate your inside committee to the employer campaign through predicting, telling stories of past campaigns and providing examples of materials from previous campaigns.

Your goal is to inoculate your committee so well, and give them so many stories and examples that they will spread the inoculation messages into the workplace.

4. EDUCATION (ROLEPLAYING)

The last part of the meeting is an education session to build up the confidence of your committee.

Don't just tell them to "recruit people to the organizing committee". Show them what to say.

Don't just tell them to "get a department to sign authorization cards". Give them a formatted employee list for the department with room to make notes and a "do's and don'ts" sheet for signing cards.

Identify some objections and questions they are likely to get as they complete this week's assignment.

INSIDE COMMITTEE HANDBOOKS

An easy way to build the confidence of the inside committee is to create a handbook for your inside committee. This is essentially a guide for how to organize a workplace in a particular industry.

The guide should contain a number of things:

1. THE ORGANIZING GAME PLAN

Explain the organizing model, or game plan, that your union runs during an organizing drive.

Explain the process for identifying leaders, building an inside committee, building a list, card signing, and winning votes.

The inside committee guide should show the benchmarks a campaign must meet to continue. When will you file? What establishes when you move into the card signing stage?

Having the benchmarks in print establishes your credibility setting benchmarks as an organizer.

You are demonstrating that you know what it takes to win.

2. TESTIMONIALS

Your inside committee handbook should contain testimonials and stories from workers who have joined your union in the past.

You want to demonstrate social proof that joining a union isn't that uncommon of an event.

Tell the stories about how people have come before, stood together, and won.

The testimonials should cover each of the stages of the organizing campaign. What did former inside committee members learn about building committees, card signing, and votes?

3. EMPLOYER CAMPAIGN EXAMPLES

The dirty tricks pulled by union busters in campaigns are so outrageous that they can be hard to believe.

Your committee handbook should contain leaflets from employer campaigns.

When your organizing committee sees the material, the employer campaign becomes more real and it makes them take it seriously because they have context to understand it.

4. FREQUENTLY ASKED QUESTIONS

The last thing needed in an inside committee handbook is a section for questions and answers. These should contain things the inside committee might be wondering about as well as questions they are likely to be asked as committee members by their co-workers.

Your committee members need succinct answers that show confidence on questions like:

- How does the union work?
- Where do union dues go?
- How can I be sure that the employer won't find out?

CHAPTER FIVE: COMMUNICATING OUR MESSAGE

HOW WE TALK ABOUT JOINING A UNION MAKES A DIFFERENCE

Certain messages appeared in successful organizing drives that did not appear in unsuccessful campaigns.

The researchers discovered that organizing drives that focused on values like respect, fairness, dignity, justice and a voice at work were more successful than campaigns that focused on grievance procedures, wage increases, or individual workplace problems.

When we share the values at the heart of our movement, we will find and attract other workers who share our values.

SIMPLE MESSAGES WIN

The best organizing drives are those that deliver simple, relevant and valuable messages.

There is a lot to know about the organizing process, and when creating a leaflet, you may find yourself being tempted to include everything you know.

This leads to organizing leaflets crammed with text or at worst, multi-page leaflets.

They focus on facts and logic rather than on values.

This approach is correlated with lower organizing win rates.

You train people to see your campaign messages as either important or unimportant. If you are putting out a leaflet each day or a couple times a week, then it is likely that you are over communicating with the workforce.

SPEAK ABOUT VALUES

When we speak about the values that underpin the trade union movement such as dignity, respect, justice, a living wage, or a fair day's pay for a fair day's work, we will attract workers who share in our values.

It is easy for a union buster to respond to a demand such as, "We should get a 30 cent wage increase." It is much harder to respond to "Everyone should be paid fairly for the work that they do."

If you put out a leaflet that says, "It's time to treat people with respect," and management responds by saying, "We do respect our employees," you win.

By reacting and responding they are amplifying your message and giving it credibility.

People who were on the fence will start to ask themselves, "Does management always treat us with respect and dignity?"

If people don't feel treated with respect and dignity – and management responds by saying that this is a workplace with respect and dignity – they come off as out of touch.

THE BEST USE OF LEAFLETS: SOCIAL PROOF

There is nothing people respond better to than social proof.

If you've done a lot of leafleting in large crowds, you've no doubt noticed social proof in action.

If a group of people is approaching you and the first few take a leaflet, the rest of the crowd will take a leaflet as well. But if the first few people pass you by without making any eye contact it is likely you'll be ignored by the rest of the crowd as well.

The decision on whether to take a leaflet is determined by whether or not they see other people taking a leaflet.

People want to be doing what everyone else is doing; they want to be on the winning team.

At every opportunity in your campaign look for opportunities to demonstrate social proof.

What is written on a leaflet isn't as important as who is handing it out and whose picture is on it.

Leaflets should prominently name members of the inside committee, (ideally with photos). This ends all discussion about the union being a third party and more importantly helps others get on board.

Workers think, "If my coworker didn't get fired for having their picture in a leaflet, it's probably safe for me to sign a card."

USING TESTIMONIALS AS SOCIAL PROOF

You can get testimonials from your members about why they joined the union.

You could have a social proof leaflet at the beginning of the campaign inviting people to join the organizing committee.

Midway through a campaign you could have a leaflet with testimonials from workers explaining why they signed a card.

At the end of the campaign create a leaflet with photos of workers holding up signs that say, "I'm voting yes".

5 KEYS TO GREAT LEAFLETS:
1. HAVE ONE KEY MESSAGE

What is it that you are trying to say?

Avoid putting too much information in a small space. People don't respond to complex or multiple messages in a communications piece.

If you can't summarize in one sentence what the leaflet is about, it is likely you are trying to say too much.

2. USE IMAGES TO COMMUNICATE YOUR MESSAGE

The best images are almost always images of your own members or members of the inside committee.

A good best practice is to put together a collection of member photos and cartoons for using in your leaflets.

4. TALK ABOUT THE WORKERS AS A UNION, NOT THE UNION AS AN ORGANIZATION.

Not many people are interested in joining a union because it was founded over 100 years ago.

In general, workers don't join unions in order to become trade unionists, they join because of the concrete situation at their particular workplace.

Talk about that situation as much as possible, and the specifics that workers face.

Talking about yourself is a good way to be labeled as a third party.

CHAPTER SIX: THE CARD SIGNING CAMPAIGN

RECOGNIZE CARD SIGNING FOR WHAT IT IS

Card signing isn't the organizing drive itself – it is a stage of the campaign necessary to get the union that you help build legally recognized.

Here is the minimum that you should have together before you move forward with card signing:

1. FULL EMPLOYEE LIST

Do not start your card signing campaign until you have a full employee list of every department.

If your inside committee is unable to get an employee list of a department, it is unlikely they'll be able to sign up that department either.

When you have a full list you can control the tempo and flow of the campaign. Start card signing without a full employee list and you are sure to run into costly surprises down the road that will interfere with your campaign plan.

2. INSIDE COMMITTEE SET UP

Before you start card signing you must have your inside committee fully setup and workplace leaders identified.

Having a solid inside committee and developed workplace leaders is the key to running the card campaign as quickly as possible.

Identify and speak to leaders prior to starting the card campaign.

If you seek out a leader after you start the card signing process they might feel left out.

3. BUY IN FROM YOUR INSIDE COMMITTEE

Your inside committee must have buy-in on the criteria to file is reaching 60% of cards signed.

You need to have the buy in before you start the card signing campaign because when the card signing campaign gears up so will the employer's resistance.

The pressure will start to impact your inside committee members and to take this pressure off they will urge you to file as soon as you meet the legal minimum requirement.

WHAT TO DO WHEN CARD SIGNING SLOWS DOWN

If card signing dries up, it is usually because you haven't found all the workplace leaders yet.

Working harder and putting more effort into card signing as an organizer won't lead to more cards. The only thing that will work is finding and building workplace leaders.

SPEED COUNTS

The faster you get through the card signing stage, the more likely you are to be successful.

Much of a union buster's campaign is built around stopping people from signing authorization cards. If they have a several month union-avoidance campaign ready to go and you sign up the workplace in two weeks, you'll throw them off their game.

They'll still have more messages that they want to deliver and more lies to spread – but now you've taken them into the election stage of the campaign.

A rapid card signing campaign also helps you win the election itself.

Drawn out card signing campaigns suck the enthusiasm out of the workplace. Quick campaigns generate excitement and momentum that can propel you into your election campaign.

THE UNION CARD

Did you know that what your card looks like can actually help you win more union organizing drives?

What is a union authorization card really?

Yes, it is piece of paper required by most labour boards to get to an election process – but it is also a communications piece.

For many workers, this piece of paper might actually be the first communications piece that they've seen from the union. You need to make sure it is good and that it gets your point across.

Some unions design their cards considering only the legal regulations and requirement of the labour board.

If your union card looks like a tax form rather than a communication piece, you're missing a huge opportunity.

Here are some additional things you can put on your union

card to get more organizing leads:

1. WEBSITE

Ideally workers will sign the card right away when they get them from the inside committee, but if that doesn't happen at least provide the worker with an option to get more information.

The website you link to shouldn't be your main union website or even your website to encourage people to organize a union at their workplace. The site should be a frequently asked questions type page that contains the union's key messages for workers considering signing a card.

Ideally this website will be targeted to this specific organizing drive.

2. ISSUES

Provide a space for workers to specify what matters to them personally. Perhaps a series of checkboxes or even a blank line to write issues.

There are a few key advantages to asking for issues on your organizing cards:

First it solidifies to a worker what a union actually means.

When a worker checks off boxes for "respect", "fairness", or "benefits" on a piece of paper, they are accepting that a union can get them respect, fairness or benefits at work.

Most people don't join unions for the sake of trade unionism; they join because of specific issues and concrete problems at work.

Secondly the answers from the checkboxes or blank lines provide great material for solidifying your vote prior to the election.

If someone checked off the benefits box on the card as their single most important issue, you can address their hot button issue specifically when pulling the vote.

"I know that getting health benefits is a key reason why many people joined on to organize a union here but if we're going to win a benefits package then we need people to vote yes for the union on Wednesday"

3. PERSUASIVE TEXT AND REASSURANCE

In my book "Promoting Your Union", I told organizers about the results from a series of experiments on union websites.

One of the experiments showed that adding the phrase: "You cannot be fired or disciplined for joining a union" dramatically increased the number of people who filled in the application form to be contacted by a union organizer.

Another experiment showed that similar results could be achieved by adding a final persuasive message right above the online form.

It is likely that the same applies to union cards.

Your cards should reassure people that signing is confidential and their employer will not find out.

CHAPTER SEVEN: HOUSE CALLS AND ONE-TO-ONE MEETINGS

HOUSE CALLS WORK

We may all know that house visits are a key part to the organizing process, but the survey of NLRB elections showed that less than 50% of applications had house called the majority of the unit.

The campaigns that incorporated door knocking into their campaign had a win rate of 53%.

Campaigns that did not use house calls had a win rate of 46% - a difference of 7 percentage points.

TALE OF TWO CAMPAIGNS

Lets say you had to pick which of these two campaigns would have a higher win rate.

One drive signed up 60% of the workforce, the other signed up 70% of the workforce.

All other things being equal – which campaign has a better chance of success?

Well the answer is obvious. More of the worksite signed up generally means a better election result.

But take the same example again, except this time the 60% of cards were signed up by using house calls and the 70%

campaign had collected the cards in the parking lot.

No contest.

NOT ALL CARDS ARE EQUAL

Cards that come around because of house calls are stronger cards.

When you have a meeting with a worker one on one or a member of your inside committee meets the worker at the home, the card as a result of a much longer and in depth conversation is more valuable.

Even if you can get cards through other methods, there are still good reasons to door knock the majority of the unit.

INVOLVING EVERYONE IN THE PROCESS

There is value in meeting people who will never sign a card.

- What do the non-supporters feel?
- Are there different issues important to them?
- Are there misconceptions they all seem to have?

Genuinely listen and treat the non-supporters with respect. You may never be able to get them to sign a card, but by making a connection you may be able to stop the non-supporter from being recruited to lead the anti-union campaign.

It's easy for the employer to get non-supporters riled up to demonize and spread rumors about a faceless union. It's much harder to believe slander about someone who took the time to genuinely listen to you and treated you with respect.

DRAWING OUT ISSUES

Even if house calls weren't associated with a 7 point difference in win rates, it would be worth doing them for their ability to draw out issues at the workplace.

Getting authorization cards is only the first step. After you'll have to win the vote, win a first contract and potentially win a vote to back up your demands with action.

Union organizing isn't about cards – it's about relationships. House calls allow you to build the relationships needed to win the election, strike vote and first collective agreement.

THE UNION ORGANIZER SHOULD RARELY HOUSE CALL

Paid union organizers should be the last people who ever house call.

Your role as an organizer is to organize yourself out of a job.

Never do anything for your members or the inside committee that they can do themselves.

As an organizer you can't be everywhere at once. You need to delegate your tasks, giving more responsibility to people who succeed and picking up those who fail.

YOU AREN'T THAT GOOD AT HOUSE CALLS ANYWAYS

Not you personally. If you are a staff organizer from a union, it is likely that on a personal level you are excellent at house calls.

But staff organizers don't make as persuasive house callers as workplace leaders or volunteer member organizers.

COUNTERING THE THIRD PARTY LABEL

One of the best defenses against the charge of being labeled a third party is to have inside committee members and volunteer organizers doing the work.

The union buster is going to come out with a campaign warning workers that "high paid professional union salespeople will come to your door and twist your arm to join a union"

Don't fall into their trap.

When workers see that it is their own co-workers or existing members of the union volunteering their own time you'll be able to sidestep the third party nonsense.

AN AGENDA FOR GOOD HOUSE CALLS

In a campaign you'll run different types of house calls.

At the beginning you'll be door knocking to recruit an inside committee.

Midway through the campaign is about collecting cards and finding supporters to file an application.

The end of the campaign is about solidifying your vote.

But in each stage of the campaign your door knock can be broken into six parts. Introduction, asking questions, educating and providing a union solution, collecting information, inoculation, and getting a commitment.

1. INTRODUCTION

The introduction and rapport building is one of the most important skills to master in door knocking.

When you show up at someone's door, they are immediately asking themselves, "Who is this person and why are they here?"

You need an introduction that disarms the defensiveness and gets you in the door to have a real conversation.

You can't have a discussion about something as important as forming a union through an intercom or a screen door.

You need to have a conversation and genuinely listen – and the only way to do that is if you earn their trust to come inside to talk about the issues.

One of the best ways to introduce yourself is to ask for an opinion. People love to give their opinions and love to talk about their situation at work.

You might say something like, "Hi, I'm Jason from the Care Aide Workers Union. I was contacted by a few of your co-workers who said that there have been some problems recently because of a new manager. They wanted to talk about forming their own union at their workplace, so I agreed that I'd go around and see if I could learn a little bit more about what people think. May I come in for a sec?"

A mistake that some new organizers make is to skip the opinion and ask for a commitment straight away. The first words out of their mouth essentially communicate, "are you going to sign a card or not?"

2. ASK QUESTIONS AND LISTEN

After you've gotten in the door and broken the ice, the next step is to learn what is going on at the workplace.

A mistake some organizers make is to jump straight to the union solution. They talk about how a union works and how a union can help without establishing what is actually happening at the workplace.

Make sure that your questions are genuine and that you are paying close attention.

- What is it that everyone cares about?
- What does this particular worker care about?

Be sure to note any "hot button" issues that may exist for a particular department or a particular worker.

3. EDUCATE ABOUT A UNION SOLUTION

Now that you've learned more about the worker and found some hot button issues, the next step is to educate a worker about a union (or collective) solution to the problem.

You should use the specific hot-button issues that the worker raised in context of how a union works.

The important part about the education stage is "education". You aren't a salesperson. You aren't there to convince people of anything. Your role is to help people learn more about the union so that they can organize their own workplace.

Ultimately they are the only people who can do it. Your job is to provide them with information and guide them along the process.

4. INFORMATION GATHERING

Prior to asking someone to sign a card you should look for an opportunity to gather more information.

"Those are interesting points you've raised. Are there other people who feel the same way in your department?"

"I'm trying to reach as many people as I can in the next few days to learn what people think about the idea. Is there anyone you think I should speak with?"

By providing information to the organizer they are becoming involved in the process and taking ownership.

Requesting a small ask, information, is a good small ask to use as a trial before you ask for the larger commitment - be it signing a card, joining an inside committee, wearing a union button etc.

5. INOCULATION

Inoculation to the employer's campaign should be part of every house call.

Workers are far less likely to fall for an employer trick if they know about it ahead of time.

If knowing that an employer will hold a captive audience meeting scares the worker out of supporting the union, it's better to know that now rather than having them sign a card and having them back out when the first captive audience meeting occurs.

6. GETTING A COMMITMENT

The last part of any house call is getting a commitment:

- It could be signing a card
- Joining the inside committee
- Voting in favor of the union

SHOULD YOU MAKE AN APPOINTMENT BEFORE A HOUSE VISIT?

The point of a house call is to have a serious face-to-face conversation about forming a union at the workplace, rather than over the phone.

When you call workers to set up an appointment to visit them and discuss the union, they'll often try to have the conversation you should be having face to face while they have you on the phone.

Once someone has engaged you in the conversation over the phone, it can be tough to get an appointment and you've wasted your opportunity to make a person to person connection.

MEETING MORE PEOPLE

It can be difficult for your volunteer organizers and inside committee to meet a lot of people each night if you are trying to set up appointments first.

People can be late for appointments. Sometimes they flake out on the appointment leaving you wasting your time in a coffee shop. And sometimes they'll ask you to drive to the other side of town when you might already be in a neighborhood near many of their co-workers – leaving you spending your time driving rather than meeting people face to face.

EXCEPTION TO NOT MAKING APPOINTMENTS

In general, when you are organizing workers that see themselves as highly educated or professionals, it is better to call ahead.

If you absolutely must call first before doing a house call, try to be in the area before you call to make the appointment.

Being close to the worker when you call lets you avoid crossing town several times and often means you will be able to get an appointment in the next 10 minutes.

Call them on the phone. Once they agree to the meeting, ask them where they live and say, "Hey I'm meeting with many of your co-workers today and I'm just down the street from you why don't I swing by now."

CHAPTER EIGHT: WINNING THE BOSS FIGHT

When the employer first learns about the organizing drive and starts their anti-union campaign, any misstep will hurt your win rate.

Here are some mistakes to avoid during the boss fight:

1. RESPONDING TO THE EMPLOYER'S CAMPAIGN

When you respond to the employer and counter his message – you will end up amplifying the employer's message at the worksite.

For example if the union buster distributes leaflets saying that joining a union will inevitably lead to violence, most people will ignore it as ridiculous.

But if the union organizer responds with their own leaflet on violence to counter the employer, you give his message credibility that it does not deserve.

There may be people who hadn't heard of the employer's smear campaign in the first place, and by repeating it you may be spreading the message.

The best way to win a fight with the union buster is to force the employer to respond to you rather than the other way around.

2. FAILING TO TAKE AWAY A UNION BUSTER'S BEST TACTICS

You shouldn't leave any available tactic open to a union buster that you haven't inoculated the workers against.

The best weapon you have against an employer's interference and manipulation during an organizing campaign is telling workers what their boss will do ahead of time.

Tell workers in advance that their boss will hire a union buster and about the tactics they can expect to see in the campaign so that they can prepare for them.

This way when the union buster tries to use their best fear tactics the workers will not be afraid.

The power of the union buster isn't in the threat itself – it is in the surprise – in the panic it creates – in how it distracts the union from its message.

3. GETTING INVOLVED IN A PAPER WAR

Each time the employer puts out a leaflet or sends a letter to the houses of workers, you'll feel a strong temptation (or perhaps pressure from above or from the inside committee) to put out a similar leaflet or letter in response.

If the employer talks about issues X, Y and Z – you'll want to tell people what the union would do about issues X, Y and Z.

If you start to throw paper around all over the place, workers will start to tune it out, treating it all as noise or propaganda.

When workers start to ignore communications from both sides, ultimately it is the union that loses because it distracts people from the important issues.

4. TALKING ABOUT "THE UNION" RATHER THAN WORKERS' ISSUES

Never talk about the union as an abstract organization.

Your leaflets and communications pieces must be about the issues at the workplace. They must be about the workers, not about your organization.

Communications pieces that talk about "the organization" rather than the workers specifically play into the employers hand suggesting that the union is a third party – separate and apart from its members or the inside committee.

5. USING UP YOUR BEST MATERIAL BEFORE THE CAMPAIGN IS OVER

Don't find yourself at the end of the campaign with nothing hard hitting to say.

Your battle with a union buster is a marathon not a sprint. Save some of your best messages and some of your best communications pieces for later in the campaign so that you have something left when you need to get your last few cards or build momentum prior to the vote.

PROTECT YOUR SUPPORTERS DURING THE BOSS FIGHT

Surveys indicate that people would prefer to work at a workplace with a union contract.

What prevents them from moving forward in organizing their workplace is fear. Fear or being fired, fear of being disciplined, fear of being singled out.

While it is completely unacceptable that anyone should have to worry about being fired or discipline for exercising a right they have by law – it is unfortunately the reality that we must deal with. Employers often will punish workers for exercising their legal rights and for standing up for themselves.

PLAYING IT SAFE IS RISKY

The best way to protect your card signers and your inside committee is to force them to take risks and not let them "play it safe."

While this advice sounds paradoxical, preventing workers from playing it safe is the best way to ensure there are no firings or discipline without cause during the campaign.

GIVING THE EMPLOYER PLAUSIBLE DENIABILITY

Often during the initial meeting with a union organizers - workers are under the impression that the union organizer will "organize their workplace."

They think the organizer will go out as a stranger and signup the whole workplace while the inside committee hides, preventing anyone from knowing they support the organizing drive.

Of course this is the most dangerous thing that the inside committee can do.

The employer will eventually find out who the supporters are at the workplace and perhaps even who called the union.

The employer will fire the union supporters and then claim with a straight face that these people gave the employer no indication they were union supporters and the dismissals were for an entirely different reason - not at all motivated by anti-union animus.

PUT THE INSIDE COMMITTEE INTO THE OPEN

One of the first messages that you need to give the inside committee is that the best way to protect themselves once the campaign goes into the open is to be visible with their support.

They need to be so visible that there is no chance the employer can say they were not aware they were union supporters.

They need to be so visible, vocal and open that even the slightest move against any of the inside committee members will be seen as being motivated by anti-union animus.

THE PROTECTION LETTER

Another way to push your inside committee to be as open and visible as possible is the "protection letter."

At the first inside committee meeting the organizer tells committee members that the way we protect committee members is by mailing a letter to the employer from the union making it clear that we will pursue any actions against a committee member for exercising their right to join a union. The protection letter also lists the members of the inside committee.

Sending out the protection letter does two things:

1. It discourages the employer from taking any action against your inside committee.

2. It puts your inside committee out in the open.

Once their name is in a letter to the employer, there is no hiding from that point on.

Suddenly committee members will be less afraid about having their name on a leaflet, going door knocking or handing out leaflets outside of the workplace.

The union buster knows that the more visible the union supporter – the harder it will be for him to get away with firing or disciplining the supporter.

THE BEST PROTECTION

The best protection working people have isn't the labour board, it is each other.

You can't rely on the labour board to protect workers – the only thing that you can rely on is mass support and power.

Having your inside committee play a visible and leading role in the campaign is how you can build this power.

MAKING THE UNION BUSTER PLAY DEFENSE

Putting the union buster on the defensive is the best way to make sure they don't get a chance to run their campaign of fear, promises and intimidation.

USING THEIR OWN WORDS

Find policies and quotes from the employer that back up your campaign for fairness and respect.

Directly quoting the employer will drive them nuts.

I was involved in an organizing drive where we found a management training manual that detailed appropriate conduct between managers and their employees.

One of the sections specified that managers were to treat employees with dignity and respect.

Rather than putting out a leaflet that said, "You should be treated with dignity and respect by management" we put out a leaflet that quoted the management training manual regarding dignity and respect and said that management wasn't following their own policies.

The employer was put into a tough position.

They were forced to respond because we were quoting one of their policies but how could they respond?

They could respond either by defending the policy or explaining that the quote was taken from the policy book out of context.

Neither option was a good one for the union buster.

The employer did end up responding to our message. They came off as looking weak as they were backtracking on their own policy – and by responding they ended up repeating our message of dignity and respect which gave our campaign more credibility.

ORGANIZE QUICK HIT CAMPAIGNS AROUND WINNABLE DEMANDS

A third way to go on the offensive and force union busters to respond to you is to campaign for small "no-brainer" demands.

I was once working on an organizing drive at large hotel. At an inside committee meeting one of the workers from the kitchen told us that most of the knives they have to work with are too dull and it was making it hard for kitchen staff to do their job. They had raised the issue with the kitchen manager who never got around to ordering new knives.

Later that week we put out a leaflet to kitchen staff with the demand that management buy sharper knives.

This put management in a tough position:

They could respond by getting sharper knives for the kitchen staff. But by doing so, they would prove that there is power in a union and this would strengthen our campaign.

Alternatively they could ignore or refuse the very reasonable demand. But because the demand is so small and was something that would benefit both the employer and the kitchen staff it would appear that management was out of touch with the workplace.

In the end they refused to get sharper knives for the kitchen staff, which showed the workers that management would not listen to them until they had a union.

There are two keys to quick hit campaigns:

1. It must be a small ask, concrete, widely felt and a win-win for management and the workers.

"Improve safety" isn't a good quick hit campaign, but a demand to install a guardrail in a dangerous location might be.

"Pay cashiers more" isn't a good quick hit campaign, but "do this year's performance reviews on time" might be.

"Improve patient care" isn't a good quick hit campaign, but "put enough staff on shift to be compliment with the law" might be.

2. It must be clear to all workers that the demand is coming from the inside committee, otherwise management will make the change and take credit.

HOW EFFECTIVE IS THE UNION BUSTER'S CAMPAIGN?

A study on the impacts of employer tactics on NLRB elections found that the employer's tactics have a big impact on the win rates during an organizing drive.

Where the employer interfered by using four or fewer anti-union tactics, the union won the election 64% of the time.

When the employer used five to six anti-union tactics, the union won the election 39% of the time.

This is a drop of 24 percentage points just by stepping up their anti-union campaign slightly.

When the employer ran a more thorough campaign using 10 or more anti-union tactics, unions won only 34% of elections.

Union busters now carry briefcases rather than brass knuckles, but their intention is the same. Their interference and opposition is now less overt but arguable more effective.

THREAT OF PLANT CLOSURE

The most effective tools in the union buster's tool chest are closed door meetings and the threat of closure.

The threat of closures happens in approximately 50% of campaigns because it is so effective.

Union organizing drives without a threat of plant closure had a win rate for the union of around 51%.

In campaigns where the employer threatened to close operations the win rate for the union dropped to 38%.

CLOSED DOOR MEETINGS

While we might think of the threat of closure is the most devastating thing an employer can do to interfere with a union organizing drive – closed-door intimidation turns out to be even more effective.

Where employer uses closed door intimidation meetings as part of their anti-union campaign unions had an average win rate of 40%.

Where an employer did not used closed door meetings, the union win rate in the election was 54%.

This is a drop of 14 percentage points. For context threatening to close operations had a 13 percentage point drop.

It shouldn't be a surprise that because of their effectiveness closed door intimidation meetings are used in almost 70% of employer campaigns.

TWO TYPES OF EMPLOYER CAMPAIGNS

Employer campaigns generally pull from two play books: fear and promises.

As soon as your organizing campaign gets into the open you can expect workers to be fed a steady diet of fear and promises.

THE FEAR CAMPAIGN

The fear campaign is about strikes, violence, union dues and plant closures.

The power in the fear campaign isn't in the messages themselves – but the panic, rumors, and confusion that they cause.

THE PROMISE CAMPAIGN

The mantra of the promise campaign is "give us another chance".

"We've learned our lessons"

"We've heard your concerns"

(And by the way, here is a pay raise – no hard feelings)

As soon as the inside committee disbands and the organizer leaves town the employer returns to business as usual.

Don't underestimate the promise or fear campaign. The reason why these two playbooks are so commonly used is because they are effective.

If they've opted for either the fear campaign or the promise campaign it is likely because there is something that indicates to the union buster that this is the most effective line of attack.

WHY INOCULATION CAMPAIGNS WORK

1. INOCULATION REMOVES THE PANIC

You can't stop management from running a fear or promise campaign – but you can take away the power of these campaigns by inoculating workers against them

2. INOCULATION CAMPAIGNS BUILD TRUST IN THE ORGANIZER

Union busters tend to run the same campaign time after time.

They know what works and they stick to their playbook.

Revealing the playbook ahead of time builds trust in the union organizer.

The first time that management runs a play out of the playbook that you warned your inside committee about, you demonstrate that you've been through this before.

Your inside committee will be more willing to work with you and trust your judgment.

3. INOCULATION MAKES MANAGEMENT APPEAR INSINCERE

The power of the scripts that union busters provide to management is that they present management as rational and genuinely concerned for the workers well being.

By showing workers the script prior to management delivering their lines you reveal that management is just reading a very expensive script.

They are not genuinely concerned human beings – but merely good actors.

It causes management to come off as phony and self-interested.

KEYS TO RUNNING AN INOCULATION CAMPAIGN

Inoculation campaigns are a critical part to winning union organizing drives – but how you run them matters a great deal.

INOCULATE AT EVERY OPPORTUNITY

It is impossible to over inoculate workers to the union buster's playbook.

It isn't enough to inoculate a worker a single time to the employer's campaign as a whole because a worker is focusing on different questions at each stage of the campaign.

At the beginning of the campaign at the first inside committee meeting, a worker isn't concerned with what the employer may do several months down the road during the election campaign. Your stories and inoculation messages will not resonate until a worker has the context later in the campaign to understand them.

PREDICT, ASK QUESTIONS, TELL STORIES

There are three strategies to inoculate workers against the employer campaign: predict, ask questions and tell stories.

PREDICTING

Predicting is simply telling the inside committee with authority what is going to happen next.

You should use this tactic with activities that you are almost certain the employer will do.

For example you can be almost certain that the employer will hold closed door intimidation meetings with workers.

You can be almost certain that there will be changes at the workplace, positive and negative.

You can be almost certain there will be a captive audience meeting at some time during the campaign.

Predicting with authority is a good way to build trust with the inside committee.

TELLING STORIES

With employer tactics that you are not 100% sure will happen such as threatening plant closures, sending letters to workers houses, and setting up an anti-union committee you should not use prediction.

If you predict these events and they do not happen, you will lose credibility with your committee and they will be less responsive to future inoculation messages.

For things you are not absolutely certain of, you can inoculate by telling stories of what employers have done on campaigns similar to this one.

In inoculating workers against threats of closures, I often tell the story of an organizing drive where the company hired a real-estate agent to go through the worksite to give the impression that the company was considering selling the building.

The company would bring in potential buyers to look at the

property to give people the impression that the company was considering selling the business; but sure enough the company is still there years later.

ASKING QUESTIONS

There are some situations where it is almost impossible to predict what the employer is going to do next.

For example, you can be sure that an employer will run either a promise campaign or a fear campaign, but there isn't anyway to predict which they will run until the campaign comes out in the open.

With these types of employer tactics, the way to inoculate workers against the tactic is to ask questions.

You can ask questions like:

"When an employer first finds out about an organizing drive – they'll either try to scare you out of joining a union or try to be your best friend and ask for a second chance – what do you think your boss is most likely to do?"

"Do you think your employer is the type to take an advertisement in the newspaper?"

These questions allow you to raise the issue with your inside committee so they are prepared when they see the tactics, but don't force you to commit on the likelihood of any tactic.

COUNTERING THE "UNION IS A THIRD PARTY" TACTIC

One of the union buster's favorite tricks is to brand the union as a "third party". It is an attempt to isolate the union as something separate and apart from its members.

Putting aside the irony for a moment that management hires an outside consultant who recommends to the boss he warn people against "third parties", union organizer need an effective guard against this tactic.

1. INOCULATE AGAINST THE THIRD PARTY

As with all tactic of the union buster you need to inoculate the inside committee against it and let them know it's coming.

They've probably never heard the words "third party" come out of their manager's mouth before but for the next few months all they will hear is "third party, third party, third party."

2. HAVE WORKERS FORM THEIR OWN UNION

A strong inside committee that is genuinely leading the campaign on the shop floor is an effective counter to the third party accusation.

If the committee has a high degree of ownership and involvement in the process, management's claim that the union is a third party may even turn against them.

On the other hand if you are trying to organize the workplace from the outside, the label of the third party is more likely going to stick.

3. INCREASE THE VISIBILITY OF THE INSIDE COMMITTEE

It isn't enough for your inside committee to be involved in the process of establishing a union at the worksite, they need to be seen by their co-workers as being leaders and working to make change happen.

4. DON'T DO ANYTHING FOR WORKERS THEY CAN'T DO FOR THEMSELVES

In addition to this being good advice to win campaigns – it is an effective counter if the employer is accusing the union of being a "third party".

- Don't leaflet outside the workplace if the committee can do it
- Don't make phone calls if your committee can do it
- Don't door knock if your committee can do it

Your job as an organizer isn't to form a union for people. It's to empower your committee. It's to educate them and to give them the courage to do it for themselves.

5. MAKE IT THEIR UNION FROM THE BEGINNING

From the very first meeting you must establish with your inside committee that this is "their union" and they are organizing "their union." Make it clear that your role is as a staff person of their union and that you will help them, but nobody can make a union for them – only they can.

The ownership you give to the inside committee will lead to success. The reason why the third party argument works so well is that it seeks to destroy ownership of the process and the union from the workers.

WHEN THE BOSS BREAKS THE LAW

There are two strategies to think about when an employer interferes with the right of workers to form a union and commits an unfair labour practice.

The first is a legal strategy that you win at the labour board.

The second is a workplace strategy that you win on the shop floor.

UNION BUSTERS WILL BREAK THE LAW TO TEST THE UNION

It isn't that unusual for union busters to deliberately break the law on a small issue to see how the union will respond.

Will the union challenge it or will they let it go?

If the union buster sees that the union organizer doesn't file, he might think one of two things.

1. The union organizer and the inside committee don't have good and accurate information. This means that they can be more aggressive with their campaign and cross the boundary of legality knowing that the union won't be able to put together a case.

2. You are an organizer who doesn't file a lot of unfair labour practices because you are concerned about the cost. Again the union buster will step up their campaign and may move to discipline or fire union supporters.

GET YOURSELF A REPUTATION

Often the best approach with union busters that break the law is to file early and often on unfair labour practices as soon as you have enough information to make a case.

The best-case scenario is that your union gets a reputation for aggressively taking on unfair labour practices, which will lead to lower legal costs down the road.

It isn't enough to just SAY you have a reputation for aggressively taking on unfair labour practices. You need to make one for yourself so the company lawyers will warn the union buster about stepping over the line when facing your union.

KEEP YOUR COMMITTEE INVOLVED

It is critical that you keep your inside committee up to speed with what is happening with the legal case.

If you don't keep your committee up to date with what is happening at the labour board, they might assume you aren't actively pursuing the case because nothing is happening.

WORKPLACE STRATEGY

In addition to the legal strategy, successful organizers make a strategy for the shop floor when unfair labour practices occur.

Because your union has publicly stated that it is against the law for your employer to fire, or discipline people for joining a union - the workplace will be watching the union and inside committee to see what they do next.

During an organizing drive, workers are constantly watching to see who is stronger, the union or the employer.

Workers are asking themselves, "Can a union protect me from the employer?" or "Is the employer so strong that even if we had a union they wouldn't be able to protect us anyway."

This is why you need to make sure that your legal campaign is backed up by a workplace campaign on the shop floor.

Ask your inside committee what they think they should do on the shop floor to back up the union's legal efforts.

With an effective workplace campaign you can turn the employer's disregard of the law into a win for the union.

Point out that disrespected behavior like this from the employer is exactly why workers need a union in the first place.

If the unfair labour practice occurs close to the election – turn the employer's misstep into an election issue.

If you start to earn the reputation as someone who can turn employers breaking the law into more momentum for your union – employers advised by union busters will be less likely to commit unfair labour practices in the future.

THE ROLE OF MIDDLE MANAGERS IN AN ORGANIZING DRIVE

It is a mistake to think that workers are the only targets of the union buster's campaign.

Here are some quotes from material prepared for management by union busters:

"In over twenty years of practicing union avoidance on a nationwide basis, working with companies ranging in size from ten to tens of thousands of employees, we have invariably found that the key to successful union avoidance lies with the lowest level of supervision."

"The frontline supervisor is the employee's direct link with the company, and the person who will have the most immediate impact on his day-to-day working life."

"Union avoidance training must include impressing upon supervisors that "management" includes them, and that part of their responsibility is the maintenance of union-free status. We have found it relatively easy to convince supervisors of this."

"Supervisors are the linchpin. An employee doesn't choose a union to protect him from the company, he chooses a union to protect him from a supervisor."

It should tell organizers something that the first thing that union busters do upon arriving on the scene is go straight to the front line supervisors and middle managers.

They approach the front line supervisors and foremen and try to convince them that their aims are closer to the CEO then the workers on the shop floor. They tell them that as part of management their job over the next few months is to make sure that the union doesn't get to a vote and if it does – to make sure the vote is unsuccessful.

DELIVERING THE EMPLOYER'S MESSAGE

Many of the anti-union messages from the campaign are delivered not by management but from management through the front line supervisors.

When the employer runs a "promise campaign", front line supervisors deliver the message that "Look, these guys are good guys. So maybe they messed up, but I can tell you that this has caused them to hear you now. I'm not telling you what to do, but I think they at least deserve a chance to make things better before you go union."

The union buster knows that workers on the shop floor trust their supervisors more than upper management and that the message is more likely to stick.

When the employer runs a "fear campaign", the front line supervisors again deliver the message. The union buster knows that front line supervisors are the best people to deliver messages that cross the line so that the buster can come back and say, "This was the comment of an individual front line supervisor and he was not acting on behalf on management when he said it."

WHAT TO DO WITH SUPERVISORS

Because persuading front line supervisors that their interests are identical to upper management is a key part of the union buster's campaign – preventing this from happening is a key part of the union organizer's counter campaign.

INOCULATING THE SUPERVISORS

Where frontline managers are respected by the workers you are trying to organize, it is worth reaching out to the frontline supervisors directly.

Tell frontline supervisors, "The folks who work here are talking about forming a union. I know you are a middle manager and I hope you don't take it as anything against you personally. I'm not trying to convince you of anything, I know you can't be involved as an excluded staff person and I can respect that. They'll be making a decision through a secret ballot vote, if they'll want a union they'll vote for one and if they don't they'll vote no. Sometimes in campaigns like this, an outside management consultant is brought in who tries to encourage middle managers to interfere with the election. Just remember that if you don't feel comfortable breaking the law you don't have to do it."

WAGES OF FRONT LINE SUPERVISORS

Another approach with front line supervisors is to draw their attention to what excluded managers at unionized companies you represent make.

Tell them the simple economics that when a unionized cashier makes $20 an hour, they don't pay their managers $12 an hour.

A CAUTION

This isn't a suggestion to get close to management. This approach should only be used when workers respect their front line supervisors.

During an organizing drive union busters will ask excluded supervisors to do some things that they may feel uncomfortable with, like spying, dirty trick campaigns or even breaking the law.

If you treat excluded front line supervisors with disrespect you will drive them towards management, which is exactly what the union buster is trying to do.

DEALING WITH THE THREAT OF WORKPLACE CLOSURE

Closure threats come in approximately 50% of campaigns and can turn your organizing drive sideways in a hurry if you don't deal with them effectively.

There are three effective approaches to dealing with plant closure threats:

1. INOCULATE AGAINST THE CLOSURE THREAT

There are no silver bullets in an organizing drive except where it comes to inoculating workers against management's threats.

Plant closures need to be inoculated against specifically because they are so effective and because it is hard to do anything about the plant closure threat AFTER it is made.

It is particularly important to inoculate against closures when organizing in manufacturing or other industries susceptible to capital flight.

2. GET TESTIMONIALS ON PLANT CLOSURES

The best time to counter the employer's threat of closure during an organizing drive is before he makes it. However, if you haven't inoculated workers ahead of the fact, the second best response to the plant closure threat are video testimonials from workers who faced the threat of plant closures during a certification campaign.

The time to get these testimonials is before you need them.

Once the threat of plant closure goes out you need to deal with it immediately and do not have time to go collect video testimonials from your current members who have been through an organizing drive in the past.

3. REMIND WORKERS WHAT THEIR BOSS HATES EVEN MORE THAN UNIONS

Losing money.

Be straight up with your inside committee and remind them that the only reason the employer operates the business is to make money. If they are losing money they aren't going to keep running the business, union or non-union. They would not be fighting a union drive if the plant weren't going to stay open.

The employer may not like that you've formed a union, but they're not going to lose millions of dollars just because they don't like unions.

NEVER RESPOND TO THE EMPLOYER'S CAMPAIGN

A few years ago, I was organizing a company that operated five warehouses. We spent an afternoon leafleting outside of one of the shift changes at a single warehouse to see if we could dig up any leads that could lead to an inside committee.

The next day, management responded with a letter in which they went line by line through our leaflet giving their response to each issue.

Most employees were completely unaware of our leaflet as we'd only leafleted a single shift at one single location.

But when the employer responded to our campaign with a letter sent to each of the work sites and each of the shifts, our office was flooded with calls.

Not only does responding to the employer's message look weak, responding gives ridiculously untrue ideas more credibility than they are worth and you inadvertently end up broadcasting the employer's message box to a larger audience.

The side that is responding is always the weaker side in the eyes of the workers.

HOW TO RESPOND (IF YOU HAVE TO)

If there is something you do have to counter because it is so egregious and widespread that you need to set the record straight – it is best to do it in a round about way.

Don't put your response in the leaflet that addresses management's point line by line; find away to address the matter indirectly.

You could put out a myths and fact sheet that addresses the point as one of five items.

You could put out some testimonials from your inside committee, one of which could address the issue.

By treating the matter casually you can address the issue without amplifying the message or appearing to be on the defensive.

WHEN THE BOSS MAKES IMPROVEMENTS

There are three things you need to do, quickly:

- Take credit
- Examine motivation
- Present a union comparison

1. TAKING CREDIT

It's important to take credit for the recent improvements at the workplace because it was a union that brought about those improvements.

Your message might look like:

"For five years management has absolutely refused to budge on wage increases. Now they've given you a wage increase just because some people are saying the word union. Just think what you could negotiate if you actually had one.

2. EXAMINE MOTIVATIONS

Try to provoke a conversation at the worksite.

"We haven't got a wage increase for five years and now suddenly there is no problem. Why?"

Even those who may not be supportive of unionization can connect the dots that the employer is making workplace improvements in an effort to stop the union's campaign.

3. PRESENT A UNION COMPARISON

The reason why an unexpected wage increase works for employers to slow down organizing drives is that these workers do not regularly receive wage increases.

The employer workplace improvement is a good opportunity to educate workers about how a unionized work environment.

"It's great that your employer is so afraid of the union's support that he's provided a wage increase. When you have a union at work, you get scheduled wage increases like this one almost every year."

CHAPTER NINE: USING BARGAINING SURVEYS

35% of unions use bargaining surveys as part of their campaign and start the process of building towards a first collective agreement prior to the certification vote.

The 35% of campaigns that used bargaining surveys had a win rate of 50%. The 65% of campaigns that did not use bargaining surveys had a win rate of around 42%.

This is almost a 10 point difference.

Bargaining surveys are an effective tool to use during organizing drives because they improve your chances of winning, but there are several other reasons to use them through your campaigns

1. IDENTIFYING KEY ISSUES

Bargaining surveys can tell you what really matters at the workplace.

Your inside committee may have different ideas about what is really important at a worksite and a bargaining survey is a good tool to find out if they are right.

Very few people actually join a union for the sake of trade unionism itself. It isn't that they've always wanted to be a union member and finally the chance has come. It is almost always about the concrete conditions at the workplace. Your job as an organizer is to help find these concrete conditions and find the triggers which will make the difference in a vote.

2. ACTING LIKE A UNION

Bargaining surveys can be a great tool to find problems for an internal workplace campaign at the workplace to solve.

They give your inside committee a chance to act like a union at the workplace.

It gives committee members an excuse to meet their co-workers and talk to them about how they feel about work. The more that your committee acts like a union the more ownership it will feel for the process and the harder it will be for the employer to label the union as a "third party".

3. GETTING OUT THE VOTE

If you use bargaining surveys prior to the vote and record results in your database, you'll know the right hot buttons to ask when you are calling people to come vote.

4. RESTARTING FAILED CAMPAIGNS

These hot button issues that you identify at the workplace are helpful when you are trying to restart a failed campaign.

You can ask questions to start conversations like, "I know you were having some problems at the workplace getting performance reviews on time. Has any of that changed?"

5. FRAMING THE VOTE

A good leaflet before an election talks about the advantages of voting yes and being a union member.

A great leaflet before an election puts out a set of demands based upon what workers indicated they wanted on their bargaining survey.

"Over 90% of COMPANY workers said that the most important issues you face are benefits, pension and respect at work.

If you want to take forward these issues with an elected negotiating committee then vote yes on May 2nd.

CHAPTER TEN: ACTING LIKE A UNION

Your inside committee doesn't just need to sign cards. They need to act like a union from the first day.

The idea of acting like a union and running internal campaigns sometimes gets pushback from the organizing committee because they feel that it is the organizer's job to get the cards, get to a vote, and do all the work.

If a union is built from the outside, then it doesn't belong to the workers from the very beginning – and if they didn't build it, they aren't very likely to keep it either.

THIRD PARTY

Union busters accuse unions of being outside, third party organizations – separate from their membership.

When workers build their own union, they see through this lie.

When your inside committee acts like a union from day number one and does the work themselves, the union buster's third party argument looks nothing short of ridiculous.

LESS LIKELY TO DECERTIFY

As a skilled organizer you *can* organize from the outside.

You can get all the cards. You might even win the vote. If you're really lucky you'll win a first agreement too. But you aren't very likely to keep the unit organized for more than a few years.

The reason is that when workers act like a union they learn skills as workplace leaders.

If the inside committee can't act like a union before they are certified, then they probably won't function as a union after they are certified either.

HOW CAN YOUR INSIDE COMMITTEE ACT LIKE A UNION

1. LOOK FOR COLLECTIVE SOLUTIONS TO WORKPLACE GRIEVANCES

Dealing with small winnable issues at the workplace through collective action is one of the quickest ways to get your committee to act like a union and gain the respect of their co-workers.

Look for things like unpaid overtime or violations of labour laws that can be addressed through collective action and legal channels.

2. SURVEY THE WORKPLACE

A survey campaign is a good way to establish what a union is about and why we care about workplace issues.

The other reason why surveys are great organizing tools is that they help develop the skills of the inside committee and give them an excuse to talk to their co-workers on a union issue.

Once you have a sense of the workplace issues through surveys you can run a more effective campaign.

3. INVITE INSIDE COMMITTEE MEMBERS TO UNION EVENTS

Get inside committee members out to educationals and events your union is holding. If your union is running a course for shop stewards, or membership meetings, invite your organizing committee out to it.

Connecting with workers in the union will strengthen your committee's resolve and build up their skill set.

Having workers involved in organizing drives engage with your current members has the additional benefit of helping to create an organizing culture within your local.

CHAPTER ELEVEN: EXTERNAL CAMPAIGNS

Union organizing drives that use external campaigns or community campaigns are more likely to win than other campaigns.

17% of campaigns used some form of community campaign compared to 83% of union campaigns that did not have an external campaign.

The 17% of organizing drives that included a community campaign had a win rate of 48% compared to a 44% win rate for organizing drives that did not use a community campaign.

While a 4 percentage point change isn't a huge increase, there are other reasons to use community campaigns to go along with your organizing drive.

1. PROTECTING YOUR INSIDE COMMITTEE

Employers are notorious for threatening and harassing workers who wish to join a union.

Organizers cannot rely on the labour board alone to enforce what little protections workers have in the first place for joining a union.

External pressure campaigns can be used to try to urge employers to stay neutral through the campaign, or at least not break the law.

2. REDUCING LEGAL COSTS

Legal expenses make up a substantial portion of the organizing budget of many unions. This money comes out of face-to-face organizing time with non-union workers.

Doing the initial research and finding an employer's external pressure points can help in forcing employers who commit unfair labour practices to negotiate a solution.

3. BUILD AN ORGANIZING CULTURE

External pressure campaigns provide an opportunity to involve your current members in the organizing process.

It isn't always practical to have a large number of your members involved in doing house calls, but external campaigns to backup an organizing drive can provide an outlet for member activism and building an organizing culture.

4. KEEP THE EMPLOYER BUSY

The more time an employer spends on responding to your external campaign, the less time they have to interfere in the process dealing with whether or not workers should join a union.

5. DEMONSTRATING POWER

During a campaign, undecided workers will be looking around to see who is more powerful. By running an external campaign and engaging an audience outside of the workplace you are reaching the friends neighbors and family of the workers you are trying to reach with your organizing campaign which helps you demonstrate power.

6. NEW ORGANIZING LEADS

It isn't enough to be aggressively organizing. You also need to be visible in the community as a union that is fighting back and making a difference. Bringing an organizing drive into a community is a way to bring your message to a wider audience which will hopefully lead to more organizing leads.

DIFFERENT ASPECTS OF A COMMUNITY CAMPAIGN

Another way of looking at an external campaign is that it is just a way of engaging with the largest community to focus your power on an employer.

- An external campaign can involve paid media
- It can involve going to the media with a story about the organizing drive
- You can highlight a particular practice of an employer.
- It can include public meetings

Community campaigns are particularly important when organizing in small communities. If the community is going to be discussing the organizing drive, then your message needs to be a part of the conversation.

WHAT TO BASE YOUR COMMUNITY CAMPAIGN ON

The key to a good external campaign is good research.

On the wall of a union hall, I once saw a poster that read, "God created union researchers so that union organizers could have heroes".

You can't run a good external campaign without good research. You aren't running an external campaign for the sake of running a campaign. You need a leverage point.

Here are some areas to research:

- A company's past attitudes towards unionization
- Donation records
- A company's work in a community
- Reputation of being involved in the community
- Safety violations
- Environmental violations
- Contractors
- Suppliers
- Customers
- Corporate structure
- Company directors
- Financial agencies

The type of research you dig up will determine what type of campaign you run.

Perhaps you find out that a particular company has a great reputation in the community and seems to be a good corporate citizen. You might run an external campaign encouraging them to maintain their reputation by not interfering with the democratic wishes of employees to join or not join a union.

If the employer has a poor record, then perhaps your campaign could be, "It's time for a change" or "Clean up X company".

The more research you have on potential leverage points - the better. You need to do this research prior to starting the campaign, because if you are in the middle of a campaign it may be too late to get this information.

CHAPTER TWELVE: WINNING ELECTIONS

You've built a strong inside committee, you've signed up the workplace and put in an application – now you need to actually win the vote.

BUILD UP COUNTS

The greatest factor in winning a vote isn't the tactics you use on the day of the vote, but what you have done every day up until the day of the vote.

- Wining the vote is about having a strong inside committee
- It is about escalating momentum into election day
- It's about having open supportive leaders in the workplaces
- It's about showing social proof in support of a yes vote
- It's about showing that by standing together the union is stronger than the employer

If you didn't have the correct elements in place before you filed you won't win the vote.

PUTTING TOGETHER AN ELECTION STRATEGY TO WIN

Keeping momentum building from the day you file your application to the day of the election won't happen by accident.

It requires a strategy and a plan of action.

Building momentum means being on offense from day one and having activities mapped out for the first days (or weeks depending on your jurisdiction).

The time to put together this strategy and plan of action is before you file your application.

WHAT DOES THE CARD SIGNING CAMPAIGN HAVE TO DO WITH MOMENTUM

If your card signing campaign was quick, then you will be likely to continue that momentum to your election victory.

If your card signing campaign is long and drawn out, workers will lose faith in the process and you will have an uphill battle to fight prior to the day of the vote.

KEEP ON THE OFFENSIVE USING A BARGAINING SURVEY

Keep tactics in your pocket to pull out during the election lead up such as the results from the bargaining survey.

Immediately after you file for certification, release the results of the bargaining survey.

If you are in a jurisdiction with a short election period your message could be, "These are the changes that you'd like to see in your workplace. If you'd like to be part of a union to make these changes happen then vote 'yes'."

If you are in a jurisdiction with a longer period between the application and the final election you might even want to hold a vote on your bargaining proposals.

Share the results of the bargaining proposal vote prior to the election.

SOCIAL PROOF

Social proof campaigns swing election results:

- It could involve a button campaign.

- It could involve leaflets with people explaining why they are voting 'yes'.

- It could involve lunches or other activities where supporters gather together.

- It could involve reminding workers that the reason there is an election in the first place is that the majority of their co-workers have signed union cards.

Now isn't the time to talk about why people should support unions and what your union can do.

The election period is a time to show that everyone is supporting the union and voting 'yes'.

PREPARING FOR THE FINAL LIE

Inoculation must happen through every stage of the campaign, but the one inoculation you cannot afford to miss is the inoculation against the union buster's final dirty trick.

It's becoming more common for employers to spread an outrageous lie a day or two before the election knowing that there is no way for the union to respond and correct the message before election day.

Your only defense is to tell workers to expect it.

Be sure the employer is aware of your inoculation message about the final dirty trick.

If you do this right, the employer may not try to pull off a dirty trick. If this happens you win because the employer has given up the biggest tool they have in their tool chest.

HAVE YOUR OWN LAST MINUTE PROVOCATION

The way for an organizer to take advantage of the timing of elections is to issue a last minute provocation that the employer feels compelled to respond to. (The chapter on the boss fight contains a number of examples of provocations you can use).

Forcing the employer to respond to your provocation 2-3 days before the election means you will throw the union buster off of his script of fear and promises during the time where he needs to be delivering it the most.

HOW TO ORGANIZE ELECTION DAY

How you organize yourself on the day of the election has an impact on your win rate.

Divide your organizing team into two teams.

Your inside organizers should be assigned to scrutinize the vote.

They record who has come to vote so far and then emails or text the information back to your head office so that you can track who has voted.

This team is also responsible for monitoring for unfair labour practices. Employers often will save a dirty trick for the day of the vote and your inside scruitineer could be an important witness.

The people you assign to this team should be some of the friendliest organizers on your organizing team. They should smile and greet people if they can when they come in as well as make contact.

Studies of political elections show that 15%-20% of people make the decision about who they are going to vote for after arriving at a polling station.

Make sure the last interaction they have with the union before they vote is a positive one.

OUTSIDE TEAM

Your outside team is stationed at the union office. They phone people who haven't voted, do house visits, and keep in touch with your inside committee to see what is going on. They coordinate drivers who make sure that supporters have a way to get to the poll.

Even if you are a one-person organizing department, you should get another person to help you on the outside campaign.

Votes are sometimes won or lost by one vote, and you can't afford to be careless after months of work.

CHAPTER THIRTEEN: FOLLOWUP CAMPAIGNS

Organizing drives are often won on the second time around.

Sometimes workers believe the employer's "give us another chance" campaign.

Sometimes you get a bad decision at the labour board.

And sometimes we lose campaigns that we really should have won.

QUALITIES OF A GREAT FOLLOW-UP SYSTEM

A follow-up system keeps in touch with your contacts from campaigns that were not successful the first time around.

GREAT FOLLOWUP SYSTEMS ARE SYSTEMATIC

They don't rely on an organizer remembering to pull open a file from an unsuccessful campaign. They run 24/7, not just when the organizer runs out of organizing leads.

GREAT FOLLOW UP SYSTEMS ARE AUTOMATED

They don't take a lot of time out of the organizers schedule. The organizer loads the worker and campaign information into the system once - at the end of the organizing drive, and turns off the system when a campaign starts.

GREAT FOLLOWUP SYSTEMS ARE SCHEDULED

They occur regularly and send more (and different)

information to workers who were involved in an active campaign two months ago than an organizing campaign from two years ago.

GREAT FOLLOWUP SYSTEMS DELIVER VALUE

The message to a non-union worker can't be: "Ready to join a union yet? No? Okay, I'll check again in a month." They deliver messages workers actually want to hear like industry news, job information, op-eds about the sector by your union president, and invitations to union educationals and events.

WHY HAVE A FOLLOWUP SYSTEM?
1. FOLLOW-UP SYSTEMS REMOVE BURNT TURF

One of my most frustrating moments as an organizer is sitting down with an organizing lead and having them tell me stories about "a union was around here once."

These stories involve an organizer showing up at the workplace, handing out some cards and escalating the campaign.

The campaign stalls and the organizer disappears never to be heard from again.

Organizing drives should be easier to win the second time around because you have more information and an existing relationship – but campaigns are actually less likely to win the second time around because of burnt turf.

2. "ACCIDENTAL" SALTING

Most people view the opportunity of keeping in touch with your main contact at a workplace in case things change and the contact feels its right to run another organizing drive.

The bigger opportunity involves workers who switch jobs and move to a different non-union employer.

Consider card signers other than your main contact.

These are people who:

- Like your union and supported an organizing drive
- Work in your sector
- Are likely stay in the sector if they find a new job

If you contact all card signers in a systematic way rather than just your main contact you are likely to get a hold of a union supporter who has just moved to a new workplace and can help you start a campaign.

Union organizers need to fundamentally change their relationship with workers who have signed union cards.

The labour movement's current mode of operation is that the day the campaign ends, we say to supporters of our union: "Call me again if you want to ever join a union" and drop the relationship.

It isn't unreasonable to think that someone who stayed on the sidelines during your initial campaign could be the spark for a new campaign or that they might change jobs and be interested in organizing their workplace.

3. TIMING IS EVERYTHING

There are windows of opportunity where workers want to join the union after a misstep of the boss.

By staying in constant contact with workers, you don't have to worry about missing one of those opportunities.

People might not be ready to join a union yet, but they may give you a call just to tell you what's happening at the workplace. You can use this information to find the prime opportunities to start a campaign.

Otherwise you're just relying on one particular worker to call you from the worksite and while that particular worker might be interested in organizing a union again, just because one person is interested, it doesn't necessarily mean it's a good time for the unit.

THE FIRST FOLLOW UP

First impressions are everything and this also applies to what you do in the first 30 days after being unsuccessful on a campaign.

What you do in this period will determine more than anything else if you leave burnt turf and if you'll have a good chance at organizing the unit the second time around.

1. A LETTER FROM THE PRESIDENT

You should send card signers a letter from the president thanking them for their help on the campaign.

The message should let them know that the union is still there for them and that not all campaigns are won the first time around.

The letter should come from your president rather than the organizer to demonstrate that there is a larger organization that isn't going anywhere the next time they'd like to form a union at their workplace.

If your jurisdiction has time-bars against subsequent applications, the letter should outline the process and timeline when a campaign can be run again.

A different more personalized message should be sent to members of your inside committee.

2. SOCIAL EVENT WITH INSIDE COMMITTEE

It is important to remain sensitive to the personalities around the organizing committee. They may be upset or discouraged after spending months of their time and effort on a cause that wasn't ultimately successful.

You can't afford to leave burnt turf at a workplace but you REALLY can't afford to have your inside committee left cynical or discouraged.

They weren't able to throw the knock-out punch, but not all fights are won in the first round.

3. EXIT SURVEYS

Your union should set up a system of exit surveys separate from the organizing department. These surveys should come addressed from someone who is sufficiently high up in the union, like the assistant to the president, but who is independent enough from the organizers that respondents will truthfully answer the questions.

The survey could ask questions like:

- Why did you voted yes or no
- What impacted your decision to vote?

- Was there anything left unanswered on your mind on election day?

Exit surveys are helpful for a few reasons:

First it is helpful to get feedback on your organizing model. If people voted no based on misconceptions about joining a union that is important to know.

The information about why people voted yes or no in the election will be helpful when re-starting a campaign, particularly if there is a new organizer assigned to the file.

CREATING FOLLOWUP SYSTEMS USING SOFTWARE

These types of followup systems can be set up in Microsoft Access or Outlook to remind you to contact workers on a fixed basis in the first 30 days and on a more infrequent schedule after that.

Email followups can be programmed into systems such as Aweber, Constant Contact, Vertical Response, Office Auto Pilot, ACT!, or Mailchimp. Once these systems are set up you don't have to program them again.

To watch a free video series on setting up an automated followup campaign visit

http://www.PromotingYourUnion.com

CHAPTER FOURTEEN: INVOLVING MEMBERS IN ORGANIZING DRIVES

What does involving members have to do with winning more campaigns?

A survey of NLRB elections found that 27% of union organizing drives that got to an election used member organizers compared to 73% that did not.

The win rates between the two campaigns was noticeable.

The 27% of campaigns that used member organizers won 52% of the time.

The campaigns that did not use member organizers won 42% of the time.

Put another way, campaigns that used member organizers saw a 10 percentage point boost to their win rate.

Paid staffers aren't the best people to represent an organizing drive door to door during house calls. The research indicates that members do better. Your question as an organizer is how to identify, train and use member organizers.

IDENTIFYING MEMBER ORGANIZERS

- People want to contribute

- They want to be a part of something

- They want to have ownership

These are all things that people can achieve by being a member organizer that they can't get from attending a membership meeting.

Unions have tried doing things like putting a notice in their newsletter that says, "If anyone wants to help out on an organizing drive, please call the union office and contact an organizer".

This approach doesn't work well.

There are better places to find and identify member organizers such as:

1. Membership Survey
2. Organizing Course
3. Steward base

MEMBERSHIP SURVEYS

By far the easiest way to find, identify and recruit people who have an interest in organizing is through membership surveys.

People love to give their opinion.

The survey doesn't have to be about organizing specifically, it could contain questions about your union as a whole or a survey on another aspect of your union like bargaining.

Part way through the survey you can ask questions about organizing like:

"How likely would you be to recommend someone else join the union on a scale of 1-10?"

or

"If the union was to set up a volunteer organizing committee, would you be interested in becoming a volunteer union organizer?"

People are more likely to indicate yes or provide their true feelings when they're answering a survey than if they see a notice in the union newsletter urging people to apply for a volunteer organizing committee.

After the survey, go back to the people who indicated that they would be very likely to refer people to join or interested in becoming a volunteer organizer and offer them the opportunity to get involved.

You could say, "You've indicated this is something you are interested in doing. Would we be able to get your input on this at our next meeting?"

ORGANIZING COURSES

Putting on short courses on organizing is a great way to find potential organizers and build an organizing culture in your union.

The course should cover not just how to organize, but the opportunity and the role of organizing in the union. Organizing new member's isn't just about improving the lives of new members, but it is also about building the power of existing members.

One of the major obstacles that hold people back from

volunteering as a member organizer is that they aren't quite sure what they are signing up for.

They don't yet have the confidence to volunteer.

They might have an impression of what a union organizer does that's significantly different from reality.

STEWARD OUTREACH

Your stewards, while they may not be any more or less likely to want to be involved as a member organizer, do make the best member organizers.

They can speak with confidence and authority about exactly what it means to be a member of your union.

During the boss fight the union buster will spread all sort of rumors and lies about the union. A union organizer can plead that these things aren't true, but your steward can with confidence laugh and say, "You know, I'm telling you as a member that none of that is true"

MISTAKES TO AVOID WITH MEMBER ORGANIZERS

Identifying member organizers is one thing, keeping them involved and active in campaign after campaign is another.

Here are some mistakes to avoid with member organizers.

1. THROWING PEOPLE INTO THE FIRE

Throwing people into a campaign without training to see if they succeed or don't has the lowest retention rate of any volunteer organizer strategy.

It is generally a best practice to give some sort of training either as an afternoon or weekend session prior to the first time your volunteers go door knocking.

2. GIVE THEM BORING TASKS

Avoid giving member organizers small or unexcited tasks. Have them doing house calls and face-to-face interactions as much as possible. That's what they are best at anyway.

Your job as the organizer is to do all the small stuff and preparation for them.

You are the one who should be printing off all the papers, putting things into packages, stuffing envelopes and organizing which houses need to be called.

If they come out for their first night as an member organizer and you have them doing paperwork, they aren't going to come out a second time around.

3. FAILING TO THANK VOLUNTEERS

If you are sincere it is impossible to thank volunteers enough.

Ideally you should publicly recognize the contribution of volunteers.

Thanking member organizers publicly is the right thing to do, and that is why you should do it, but thanking member organizers is also a great way to build an organizing culture in your union.

Consider having the president publicly thank them, writing an article featuring volunteer organizers, providing specific clothing or buttons to member organizers that identify them.

It will engage others in conversation, which will lead to recruiting more member organizers.

KEEPING VOLUNTEERS MOTIVATED AND COMING BACK

Don't focus on getting a member to volunteer on a single campaign. Think about how you can get them involved with five campaigns.

1. GIVE MEMBER ORGANIZERS DEFINED TASKS

People like having a defined task and responsibility. Don't just ask them to come out and be an organizer in general or have them sitting around the office.

Rather than saying, "You'll be doing house calls tonight" say, "These are the 10 people you need to reach in the next few days".

The more specific and defined a task, and more ownership that a volunteer has over the process, the more likely that a volunteer will carry it out to the fullest extent.

2. SHARE VISION

Some members may start their process of being a volunteer organizer with the impression that it is not a whole lot different from being a salesperson. The reality of course is that organizing is about building a movement; it is about building the power of our unions and empowering those who have little power.

The more that you can talk with volunteers about the role of organizing, not just in logical reasons of why a union wants member, but in terms of the values that we all share, the more motivated someone will be to come out again in the future.

3. PAINT A BIGGER PICTURE

How does a particular action that a volunteer organizer is doing fit into the larger campaign?

- How does door knocking fit into a larger campaign?
- Why do we do it?
- Why aren't paid staff doing it?

These are some things to talk about with volunteer organizers before they go out. They should understand exactly how the actions that they are taking today are building a bigger movement.

4. MAKE VOLUNTEERS INSIDERS

Give volunteers as much information about the campaign as you can, ideally some insider information. One of the best ways to get people to have a sense of ownership is to give them the feeling of being insiders.

HOW TO BUILD A CULTURE OF ORGANIZING

1. USE VOLUNTEERS ON EVERY ORGANIZING DRIVE

In addition to performing better at house calls than paid staff, having members volunteer on organizing drives gives them an appreciation of what the union does which they take back to the worksite.

2. PUT ON ORGANIZING COURSES

They could be weekend, one day or even drop in courses in

the afternoon where members have the opportunity to learn about the organizing process and find out what the union is working on right now.

The best types of organizing courses are unpaid.

They attracts people who are motivated for the right reason.

Someone who is only coming for an organizing course if there is a paycheck that goes with it isn't going to stick around for the hard work of an organizing campaign.

3. MAKE ORGANIZING PART OF EVERY THING YOUR UNION DOES

Every servicing visit should have a component where organizing is talked about on the shop floor. Your membership meetings should have a discussion about organizing.

This isn't just a 5 minute report from the organizer, but an active discussion of your members.

Building an organizing culture requires a change from the top and recognition that organizing isn't just a particular department of your union; it is a task for all members of your union.

If your union has some audacious organizing goals, they aren't going to be met by the handful of people who work in the organizing department alone.

4. REFRAME ORGANIZING

You can't talk with your members about organizing just in term of expanding the union and getting more members. To build an organizing culture that permeates the whole organization, organizing must be about building power for existing members.

Members must see how organizing directly impacts their contract negotiations, their grievances, the ability for the union to have a voice on public policy issues.

5. SET UP A VOLUNTEER ORGANIZING COMMITTEE

Have the committee meet monthly. Meetings should include presentations from the organizer on the state of the union's various campaigns. Committee members should be given tasks and assignments on doing research on targets and providing campaign feedback.

Ideally the committee should be chaired by your president, rather than an organizer. If you're serious about changing the culture of your organization then it needs to be reflected from the top in your leadership.

MEMBERS ARE AN ORGANIZERS BIGGEST ASSET

Members are critical to this process. If you are organizing an industry with tens of thousands of people, there is no way a handful of paid staff can realistically make this outreach.

Members have an understanding and knowledge of the industry that is collectively deeper than any of your staff.

They know what's going on right now, they know the trends, and all the gossip.

While organizing staff are often organizationally separated

from membership, connecting them allows organizers to build their information base and select better campaigns.

Running better campaigns at better targets improves your win rate and also gives organizers a starting point when knocking on doors for the first time building an inside committee.

TRAINING VOLUNTEER ORGANIZERS

There are a few schools of thought about the best way to train volunteers for organizing drives.

The first is that the best thing to do is send people into the fire and see how people perform sending them out cold to door knock.

The second is to do some sort of minimal training, such as a day or two of basic do's and don'ts and then send them directly into the field.

The third is to give volunteers intensive training before sending them out into the field, perhaps a week of training so that they are prepared.

The second type of training is the most likely to succeed.

It gives member a good sense of what is expected of them and gives them confidence to do their tasks. They are more likely to stick around than if you put someone through a weeklong course where they'll get too much information. They'll either be overwhelmed with the information or lack the experience or context to really understand or use the information you are providing them.

Here's what a one or two day session should cover:

1. THE LAW

You shouldn't cover the whole labour code, but you should specifically cover some of the basics about what the union can and cannot do at the workplace. Equally you should cover what the employer can and cannot legally do during a campaign.

While the advantage of volunteer organizers is that they have more credibility as a worker coming out of the jobsite, they should be armed with the basics so that they can speak with some confidence if they are asked questions about the laws by potential union members.

2. DO'S AND DON'TS

Cover the do's and don'ts of the particular task you are asking workers to do.

If you are going to do a door knocking blitz, then let your members know about best practices and things to avoid.

Once they have more confidence in their ability to do a task, they'll be more willing to stick around in the future to help organize.

3. ROLE PLAYING

There are common questions that come up in most house calls.

They include questions around how the union works, if people are going to get fired, how contracts work etc. It is a good idea to run through questions that you can anticipate before sending out volunteers for the first time.

WHAT CAN VOLUNTEER MEMBER ORGANIZERS DO?

Here are a few ways you could involve your members in organizing:

1. The best thing for members to do is house calls. Member organizers are able to build rapport and speak from experience better than paid organizers.

2. While not as valuable as house calls, phoning is another activity volunteers can help with.

3. Leafleting non-union worksites. If you use member volunteers as leafleters, it is important that you have a way to demonstrate they are a volunteer not a paid staff person. The biggest asset of member organizers is that they are volunteering their time, but if you were a non-union worker and saw them at the factory gate you might not know that this was someone volunteering their time to help you without a visual cue such as a button.

4. Get together for a night and map out the different employers in an industry, the connections between them, ownership structures, and relative locations. These maps are incredibly useful for organizers and researchers. After mapping employers of an industry ask a worker what friends they have at the workplace.

VIDEO TESTIMONIAL CAMPAIGNS

Through an organizing campaign, the biggest obstacle to workers uniting is fear: fear of the unknown, fear of the lies they've been told by the employer.

Unfortunately you won't be able to get your members out to speak with every potential member, but you can put together video testimonials to deliver that message effectively.

Try to get testimonials for each stage of the campaign.

Get video testimonials from inside committee members of successfully organized workplaces about why someone should join an inside committee. Create testimonials on why someone should sign a card. Include testimonials on how bargaining and contracts work.

Collecting video testimonials from your members is a great excuse to talk with members on the worksite about organizing.

Once a member has provided a video testimonial about their experience in the union, they are more likely to be interested in joining the volunteer organizing committee. They will feel like they are more of a part of the union and will probably be honored that you asked them in the first place.

HOW TO GET VIDEO TESTIMONIALS

Here are four easy ways to get video testimonials from your membership:

1. SEND YOUR ORGANIZERS TO MEETINGS

Set up a camera and a backdrop outside of the meeting and try to engage members as they are going in and out of the meeting. During the meeting the organizer should make a pitch to the group to meet in the hall after the meeting and that they'd like to get testimonials from members about their experience in the union.

2. VOLUNTEER ORGANIZING COMMITTEE

Each member of the volunteer organizing committee should give a testimonial. This is a group that you can coach a little more and tell them exactly what type of a testimonial that you are looking for.

3. WORKPLACE VISITS

If you have the ability in your contract to do workplace visits this is a great way to engage your membership. You will have a lower success rate in engaging people than at a membership meeting or your volunteer organizing committee meeting, but you'll have a higher chance to run across someone amazing who previously wasn't on your radar.

4. USER GENERATED CONTENT

The last way to collect video testimonials is to hold a contest where members are encouraged to post what they like about being a union member on YouTube.

YouTube is now the second biggest search engine in the world behind Google.

Wouldn't it be great if someone was typing, "How to join a union" and they came across a video testimonial of one of your members explaining why they like being a member of your union?

CHAPTER FIFTEEN: LEARNING FROM CAMPAIGNS

WHY HAVE DEBRIEFING SESSIONS?

1. WE NEED TO LEARN AS TEAMS

Employers have almost unlimited money to throw at organizing campaigns, and no issues with ignoring the law and discriminating against union activists.

We need to make sure that we are the best we can be and that requires a system to learn and get better as a team.

2. WE DON'T LEARN FROM EXPERIENCE

There is a myth that union organizers learn from their experiences on campaigns. This isn't true. Organizers learn from reflecting on those experiences.

There are always house calls to do and more phone calls to make. If you don't schedule debriefings and structure them in a way that they are effective for your time, they won't get done.

3. SHARING OUR SKILLS AND EXPERIENCES

Left on your own, you can only learn from your own campaigns. By formalizing debriefing sessions, you can learn not just from your own campaigns but other campaigns as well.

Veteran organizers need to share their experience and wisdom with younger organizers. The huge demographic shift that is impacting the rest of the working class is happening to staff organizers as well. We must ensure that the skills learned by organizers leaving the workforce are passed on to the next generation of people coming along.

WHAT SHOULD A CAMPAIGN DEBRIEFING SESSION LOOK LIKE?

There are three things to consider:

1. Who should be there
2. When to conduct them
3. What should the agenda look like

WHO SHOULD BE AT THE DEBRIEFING SESSIONS?

The full organizing department. Field organizers, lead organizers, researchers, communications staff etc.

There are a few reasons for this:

1. Any lessons and insights learned from the experience of the campaign should be shared with the department, not just the individuals directly involved in the drive

2. It can be hard for people who have spent the last few months of their lives living and breathing the campaign to look objectively at it.

3. Having outsiders helps to create a better environment for more productive discussions. Often having an outsider can help those people working directly on the

campaign see the problems with their campaign hidden in plain sight.

If you only conduct briefing session with organizers directly involved people might get the wrong idea. Organizers might become defensive, looking to avoid blame. Bringing everyone there establishes that the point of debriefing sessions is learning not to blame.

WHEN SHOULD DEBRIEFING SESSIONS BE HELD?

If possible hold the campaign debriefing session prior to the results of the vote being announced.

Often the outcome of the election can hide many of the lessons that were in the campaign.

If the campaign was a success, but you made several mistakes, it is easy to ignore the mistakes in light of victory.

The same is true of campaign losses. The emotion of a loss can sometimes obscure the objective facts and introduce negative emotions into the debriefing sessions.

DEBRIEFING SESSION AGENDAS

The difference between doing a debrief as an academic exercise and learning real lessons to win future campaigns depends on how well the debrief is structured.

A good debriefing session has five parts.

1. Get gut feelings, emotions, initial judgments on the table

2. Review objective information, data and facts

3. Discuss the positive aspects of the campaign

4. Look critically at the campaign's negative aspects

5. Discuss what was new about this campaign and what was learned

1. INITIAL IMPRESSIONS

While its important to look at all aspects of the campaign objectively, it is necessary to give participants an opportunity to get their initial feelings out on the table.

If people hold off on expressing their initial gut feelings until later on in the debriefing session, they will sit in the meeting thinking about the one point that they would like to make later on.

This should be done as a 15 minute round table exercise, where people go around the table and say their initial thoughts about the campaign.

This isn't a spot for to debate what is correct, just to get initial impressions on the table.

2. REVIEW OBJECTIVE INFORMATION DATA AND FACTS

Before moving on to look at positive and negative aspects of the campaign, it is important that everyone is working from the same set of facts.

This should be a 15 minute part of the agenda.

Again this isn't a place for debate. The goal is to list as many objective facts and agreed upon items about the campaign as possible.

This is the time to look at questions like:

- What was the breakdown of marks?
- How often did the inside committee meet?
- How many people were on the inside committee?
- What was the makeup of the inside committee?
- How many cards were signed?
- What were the leaflets that the employer released?
- What was the momentum of the campaign at the time of filing?

3. POSITIVE ASPECTS OF THE CAMPAIGN

Next move on to a 15 minute discussion of the positive aspects of the campaign. In this section it is important to focus the group discussion – no one is allowed to talk about anything negative.

It is important to have a separate discussion about the positive and negative aspects of the campaign rather than just a general conversation because in these discussions can be tempting to focus on the positive aspects of successful campaigns and the negative aspects of failed campaigns.

4. NEGATIVE/CRITICAL ASPECTS OF CAMPAIGN

Next the group should spend 15 minutes looking critically at the campaign.

The point of this discussion isn't to be a critic for the sake of being critical.

You are looking for things that could have been done better or things that didn't quite go your way.

5. WHAT'S NEW?

Look at questions such as:

- What were the overall lessons learned?
- What have we learned about this employer's tactics?
- What have we learned about how we work together as a team?
- What have we learned about our labour board strategy?
- Have we learned any new techniques for card signing or door knocking?

MISTAKES TO AVOID DURING DEBRIEFING SESSIONS

Here are common pitfalls that hold back debriefing sessions from being effective.

1. HOLDING DEBRIEFING SESSIONS ONLY ON LOSSES

Holding debriefing sessions only after major losses will cause people to question your motives of holding a debriefing session.

The purpose of a debriefing session is to learn as a team.

If you hold a debriefing session after a loss but not normally after wins, organizers will be defensive and the session will turn into an ass-covering and blame session.

2. NOT ENOUGH TIME

You've spent the last few months and hundreds of hours on a campaign, so spend the time debriefing the campaign itself so that you don't make the same mistakes and so you apply new lessons to new campaigns.

Getting all of the ideas out on the floor and discussing them fully takes time and this costs your department money, but ultimately it is less expensive than losing a campaign from repeating mistakes.

3. FREE FOR ALL CONVERSATIONS

Free for all conversations lead to group think.

In these discussions it is hard to separate things that are objective from subjective opinions.

No one will find the mistakes of your campaign in a general conversation if you've had a resounding organizing win.

STOPPING FINGER POINTING SESSIONS

A common problem when unions first try running debriefing sessions for their organizers is that they can quickly become sessions to point fingers and make excuses. This saps any energy that could have come out of the debriefing session and takes away the learning opportunities from the organizer.

Ultimately the key to having a good debriefing session is trust. There are four things you can do to increase the trust in your debriefing sessions in order to avoid finger pointing.

1. STATE INTENT

At the beginning of a debriefing session, be upfront about the purpose. You've called together your team to learn lessons from the campaign and the intent isn't to find blame but learn for the next campaign and become better as a team.

2. REGULARIZE DEBRIEFING

Debriefing sessions must become a regular part of the culture of your team. The more regular they are, the less skeptical people will be about the sessions and the more useful will be the feedback that you will get out of participants.

Holding sessions infrequently will cause people to question your motives.

3. OFF THE RECORD

It should be made clear to organizers that in looking at mistakes, no one will be disciplined for those mistakes.

There isn't anything wrong with making mistakes – but there is problem with not learning from them.

www.ingramcontent.com/pod-product-compliance
Lightning Source LLC
Chambersburg PA
CBHW061512180526
45171CB00001B/149